We Can Do It

We Will Do It

And We ARE Doing It!

Building An Ecovillage Future

JT Ross Jackson, Ph.D.

Robert D. Reed Publishers

San Francisco

ISBN 1-885003-45-5

Library of Congress Catalog Card Number: 00-100655

Cover design by Irene Taylor, it grafx
Typesetting by Barbara Kruger

Robert D. Reed Publishers
San Francisco

"Would it be an exaggeration to claim that the emergence of the ecovillage movement is the most significant event in the 20th century? I don't think so."

—sociologist Ted Trainer of the University of New South Wales, Australia.

We can do it
We will do it
And we ARE doing it!

—rallying cry of GEN—The Global Ecovillage Network

About the Author

by David C. Korten

This book presents the personal life journey and vision of a very special human being, Ross Jackson, and his life partner, Hildur Jackson. The story gains a special power and interest from the fact that Ross leads an unusual double life. In the world of global finance he is known as the board chair of Gaiacorp, a leading manager of currency-based hedge funds and advisor to international financial institutions on foreign exchange management. In the world of environmental activism, he is known as the board chair of Gaia Trust, a visionary, grant-making foundation that has expended more than $15 million in Gaiacorp profits to support groups around the world pioneering the development of ecovillages and green enterprises as the foundation of a 21st century civilization.

Ross is one of a special circle of visionaries that includes such luminaries as Anita Roddick of the Body Shop, Dee Hock of Visa International, Paul Hawken of Smith and Hawken, and George Soros of the Quantum Fund. These are no ordinary social critics. Each rose from a modest background to achieve extraordinary success in the institutions of international business and finance. Each then moved on to share with the rest of us their insider's understanding of the destructive nature of the institutions they came to master, and lent their energies to the task of creating societies more responsive to the needs of people, community, and nature.

While it is not uncommon for successful entrepreneurs who create large personal fortunes to eventually turn their attention to philanthropy, Ross is distinctive in that he established Gaiacorp for the primary explicit purpose of generating profits to finance progressive social change. Ross is also distinctive in the ease with which he moves from sharing his personal insights into the forthcoming step to human spiritual maturity, to offering clear and informative tutorials on such topics as the causes of global financial instability and why the Tobin Tax will neither raise large revenues nor reduce financial speculation.

Ross provides a powerful insider's view of the real nature of the global economy and how it is being intentionally crafted by global corporations and financiers through institutions like the World Trade Organization to speed the wanton exploitation of labor and destruction of the planetary life support system for quick profits. He brands economic globalization a program of "shareholder protectionism," because the rules created and enforced by the WTO seek to maximize shareholder profits while passing the real costs of production onto the larger society. He calls neoliberal economics "free ride" economics, because it seeks a free ride for those who own productive assets—in direct violation of one of the most basic principles of market economics.

Ross informs us that protectionism, so long as it is protecting the interests of people and nature, is not really a bad thing. The real issue is whether global rules will protect the interests of an elite group of corporate shareholders or the interests of the other 99 percent of humanity. In the following, Ross cuts through the self-serving mantra of the free trade advocates to affirm some obvious truths that have been badly obscured by free trade ideologues.

"Of course local cultures have every right to protect themselves against foreign commercial interests whose only motive is to extract as much money as possible from the local culture. Of course local cultures should decide who should be allowed to peddle goods within their territory, without having to provide 'scientific proof' of anything. Of course local cultures should be the ones to decide under what conditions foreigners should be allowed to extract money from their society.

The true heart of this book, however, is its exposition of the possibilities within our reach to organize human spaces into ecovillages that restore our sense of community and our connection to the earth, while providing us with environmentally sound and sustainable sources of livelihood. Ross brings an uncommon sense of reality to his vision of the possible. While it contrasts sharply with the rootless, money-mad world of the global economy, it is grounded in the real experience of hundreds of ecovillage and green enterprise experiments that are being developed around the world, many of them with financial and technical support from Gaia Trust.

Though many politicians, corporate CEOs and media pundits remain in deep denial, it is evident to a growing portion of the world's population that an increasingly unstable and destructive economic system that values money more than life is leading humanity toward ecological and financial collapse. The great question of our time is whether we will find the will and the wisdom to change course before we suffer the inevitable consequences of our folly.

A spiritual experience in India, eloquently described in Chapter 4, has given Ross an optimistic view of the human future. Many readers will find the final chapter—where Ross lays out his vision of an ecovillage future in a story format—to be their favorite. Ross believes, however, that widespread change is most likely to come only after a devastating breakdown forces an end to business as usual.

I believe there is still hope we might do better. The more clearly we come to see the alternatives, the better the prospect of our making an intelligent pre-disaster choice for life. The work being done by Ross and Hildur Jackson helps us to see the nature and benefits of such a choice and may yet lead us to take the step toward a more intelligent and satisfying way of being— before we find ourselves reduced to a struggle for physical survival.

David C. Korten, author of *When Corporations Rule the World*

Author's Comments

I recall doing a term paper back in my business school days in the United States in the early 1960s, when we were asked to look into the future and identify the key problems that our generation would face. One of my central predictions was that it would be a time of great change, probably greater than anything seen in our history. A key need would be for us to be flexible, and to be open to the change that was coming. I was thinking mostly of the anticipated effects of computer technology.

But little did I realize how true it also would be for me at the personal level. I could not foresee at the time that I would undergo a personal transformation and come to reject many of the most basic assumptions of my education, as I tried to pull together the different strands of my life into a coherent whole. As time passed, I saw more and more clearly that we—in the sense of our civilization, were embarking on a very questionable path, and many of my business colleagues were leading the way.

I eventually saw a way out—and put all my efforts behind the ecovillage movement. Ted Trainer may or may not be right in his judgment of the importance of the ecovillage movement. It is still early days. But from this vantage point, it seems to be the right initiative at the right time to deal with what I expect will become a major polarizing issue in the coming years—with an outcome vital to what kind of a future we will create for this planet—the issue of commercial globalization versus local community values.

What is special about the ideal ecovillage is that it is truly holistic, integrating all aspects of our lives in a single place, where social, environmental, and spiritual aspects meet—in a vibrant local community that can continue forever in harmony with nature. And what is special about ecovillagers is that they are not writing papers for the next conference, or philosophizing over the back fence about what we ought to do about the global crisis. *They ARE doing it,* walking their talk, blazing trail—founding a new culture for a new millennium, based on new values, or more correctly, very ancient values that are being rediscovered.

JT Ross Jackson   Copenhagen, spring, 2000

Contents

1

Getting Established

It was Cleveland, Ohio, June 1964, and clearly a watershed time in my life as I mentally prepared to leave in a few days for Copenhagen, Denmark, and unknown adventures ahead. Checking my wallet, I saw that I had just enough for my one-way ticket, and a little extra. I was pleased that my plans had worked out so well so far. Having just completed my Ph.D. in Operations Research (OR) at Case Institute of Technology (later Case Western Reserve University after a merger with the neighboring university), I was keen to get going in the business world.

The plan to go to Denmark had evolved slowly over the past few months. I had never been to Europe, but had always wanted to see a little more of the world. Deep down I had always admired people who were fluent in more than one language, and was determined to be so myself. Being 25 and single, I realized there might never be a better opportunity to travel. In addition, international business experience would be a valuable addition to my CV in any job I might seek later in Canada or the USA.

I had a close friend, Peter Pruzan, who lived in Copenhagen. We had lived together for a year in Cleveland, where he had completed his Ph.D. in the same field at Case the year before, and had then gone back to Denmark to marry a Danish girl, Vita, whom I had met the previous summer. She was a vivacious, lovely girl, who reinforced my impression of Danish girls as tall, healthy, and attractive, with a very natural way about them. Peter had spent two years as a consultant in Sweden and Denmark before coming back to the US for further studies. He was now a lecturer at the Technical University of Denmark, after being with IBM for a while. We had corresponded during the past year, and he had suggested to IBM that I take over the job he had had as an OR consultant, and they had indicated that they would be glad to take me on.

My flight to Copenhagen had a stopover in London, so I decided to use the opportunity to stay there for a couple of days. It was indeed exciting to see for the first time Piccadilly Circus, Trafalgar Square, and all the other sights, and to feel the throbbing heart of great London Town.

I had made prior arrangements to see an acquaintance—a visiting professor at Case the previous year, who had invited me to pay him a visit in Bristol, where he was a senior executive at a steel mill. That turned out to be an interesting visit in more ways than one, including another job offer. But the thing that struck me most was the "three martini lunch" that I had heard about but never experienced. The English culture struck me as significantly different from the American—much more laid back, imperial, almost decadent. I made a mental note that was to come in handy several years later when I started doing business in London—if you want to make a deal with an Englishman, make sure you do it before lunch.

On the flight to Copenhagen, I pulled out the one book about the Danish language that I had been able to find in the Cleveland public library. It was a very thin phrase book, published in 1905. I was apparently the only one to have borrowed it in the last forty years, so I had no qualms about taking it with me. I had arranged for Peter to meet me along with a colleague from IBM, and decided I would surprise them with a little knowledge of Danish. So I looked up how to say "How do you do?" and memorized the phonetic pronunciation.

Upon arrival I greeted Peter warmly, shook hands with his IBM friend, and decided to try out my Danish on them. They both howled with laughter for a long time as I looked on dumbfounded. Apparently my archaic 1905 Danish greeting was the rough equivalent in English of "How art thou?"

So we all had a good laugh and drove to Søllerød Inn for a drink and chat. We talked for a long time about everything under the sun except my job. This was my first exposure to what in time I came to realize was a typical Danish characteristic—and very unlike the American style. You don't go directly to the matter at hand, but beat around the bush as long as possible until you can no longer avoid the issue, at which time you say "By the way...."

Anyway, after a couple of hours, it was finally put to me with great apologies that there had been a major misunderstanding between Peter and IBM concerning the seriousness of my coming. Quite likely as a result of the above culture clash. After much going back and forth, the IBM man finally put it straight to me. "I am afraid we do not have a job for you."

Peter put me up at his place, and we agreed that I would stay for a couple of weeks, and that he would lend me the money for a return ticket. In the meantime, I would have a little vacation and try to talk to the head of IBM personally, according to the old adage: never take no for an answer.

My first impression of downtown Copenhagen would probably surprise many people, but it is still as clear as a bell to me. The streets were clean! One of my most negative memories of my three years studying in Cleveland was the gritting sound of soot particles as I turned the pages of my books. I detested their indifference to dirty air and paper-filled streets. I swore to myself that I was never going to live there, in spite of the fact that I had many good friends who did. I don't think I ever saw a Clevelander stop to pick up a piece of paper blowing in the wind and put it in a trash can. But I saw it in Copenhagen—many times.

I had arrived on the 4th of July in the middle of the tourist season, and enjoyed mingling with people in the street cafés, in Tivoli and in the bars. I was favorably impressed with just about everyone I met. They were very friendly, spoke excellent English, and had a very natural, modest way about them that appealed to me—especially the girls. So I decided to make an extra effort with IBM and see if I couldn't get them to change their minds.

I set up a meeting with the sales manager, who had the power to hire and fire. I was told he was a tough cookie, but that under the intimidating exterior there was a twisted sense of humor. At first glance he looked very sour and unlikely to do anyone a favor.

"So you are a friend of Peter Pruzan's," he said gruffly. "I understand he recommends you highly. We were very pleased with Peter's work, and were sorry he left us for the Technical University. As a rule, we do not hire foreign nationals, you know."

"Then how come Peter?" I asked.

"Well, he has a very special background." He paused. "The only exception we can make is if the foreign national has a specialty that is not found here," said Dyre.

"Well, I have the same education as Peter. We both specialized in Operations Research."

He raised his eyebrows slightly as if he hadn't been briefed on that, but didn't seem swayed. I continued, "I believe that the nature of using computers is shifting away from just duplicating bookkeeping functions to being used as a tool in decision-making. I could help your customers find new application areas."

This was the view of Professor Russell Ackoff, the leading authority on OR in the US at the time. He was head of the Case OR

Department and the reason I chose to do my Ph.D. there. I recalled him saying that only about 2% of computer applications at that time were for more advanced uses of computers. The rest were basically for what he called "bookkeeping." He foresaw a radical shift over the next twenty years toward more advanced uses. In retrospect, he was wrong. Thirty years later, the figure is still about 2%, although the absolute magnitudes of course are enormously higher. That revolution is still to come. But it will come eventually. Perhaps in a different way than we imagined then, with digitalization of photographs, films and computer games becoming enormous gobblers of computer capacity as we enter the era of multimedia in the 2000s. What none of us foresaw then was the way the costs of computers would fall so drastically, opening up vast new markets in smaller companies that couldn't dream of computerizing in the sixties, but their applications remained mainly in the "bookkeeping" area.

"Hmmm," said the sales manager, "And what kind of salary level would you expect?"

"About $1000 per month." That was considerably less than American levels, but what I figured was reasonable here after speaking with Peter.

He frowned. "I don't know. That's what we pay a salesman with seven years' experience." I didn't see what that had to do with it, but as he started collecting his papers and looked at his watch, I realized I was losing him. He was about to speak, and I knew what he was going to say, so I decided to make a gamble. I wasn't ready to give up just yet.

I cut him off. "Tell you what," I said. "I'm willing to work at half that rate for six months, and show you what I can do. On one condition. At the end of that time, you either fire me or double the salary."

He looked hard at me and then leaned back and smiled for the first time. "Very like an American," he said.

"Canadian."

He nodded. "OK," he said, and extended his hand. "I like a little boldness. Report to me on Monday."

IBM was a very interesting organization at that time. It was of course one of the biggest success stories of the century. Its sales organization was generally regarded as the best in the world in any branch of business—bar none. It was super-competitive, based on a quota system. Sales bonuses were based on beating your quota, and the quotas increased relentlessly year after year. And the top salesmen just went right on beating them year after year. The salesmen were the cream of the crop in every country IBM located—really top quality sellers.

Systems people—and I was put with that group, were definitely second class citizens within the organization, necessary but not as glamorous.

My job was to help the salesmen. But only if they wanted help. Most didn't think they needed any. But a few were quite keen. I often took the initiative in finding out who was trying to do what where, and picked my shots as to where I could make a contribution—normally where some kind of optimization or simulation was required, or somebody had a problem that hadn't been solved before. I was soon up to my ears in projects in many different branches. Danish companies were generally speaking a few years behind America in their use of computers—particularly regarding anything involving mathematics, so for me it was an exciting period introducing new concepts and a new way of thinking to Danish executives, who were very open to innovative ideas and quick to learn.

When my six months were up, IBM met my terms, so I stayed on, and sent a memo to my colleagues requesting all future correspondence to be in Danish. My IBM time was a very challenging and educational experience for almost two years. I got to meet a broad cross-section of the top executives of Danish commerce and industry, mostly the larger companies, who were more appropriate for my particular kind of skills.

But by early 1966 it was becoming more and more clear to me that a large organization was not ideal for me. I wanted to be my own boss as soon as possible in a small consulting operation. Peter and I talked more and more about forming a specialist consulting company, which we would call Operations Analysis Corporation, or OAC, for short. It would be the first of its kind in Denmark, maybe anywhere, specializing in OR.

In its original concept—which was the one that inspired me—OR was a multidisciplinary holistic science of decision-making. You took your starting point in the total situation and looked at it from all angles without prejudice. Its roots went back to the Second World War, where multidisciplinary teams of Allied scientists had worked together to solve operational problems in the military, and with great success. But it is a difficult concept to teach. You either think broadly or you don't. Most people don't. This is one reason why the field has since degenerated into a limited "tool-box" approach by the practitioners and to a narrow science by the academics who fill up the journals.

I first went to the chief executive and proposed setting up a consultant operation inside IBM, based on my vision that the long term future of IBM was not selling hardware, but selling software and associated consulting. This was heresy at the time because IBM was totally dominated by hardware thinking and sold its products "bundled," i.e., with standard software included in the hardware price, and almost never charged extra for system consultants. So there was no sympathy whatsoever for my suggestion, which was considered "off the wall." It may have been too early anyway, but it is interesting that IBM did eventually reach the same conclusion about its future, but not until the 1990s after the rise of Microsoft, when they were in deep trouble. When my proposal didn't fly, I began surveying my IBM contacts for potential start-up clients for OAC.

Two of the most interesting candidates were Landmandsbanken (later Den Danske Bank) and Copenhagen Handelsbank, which merged with Den Danske Bank many years later. But at the time, the two of them competed intensely with each other for the title of Denmark's largest and most progressive bank. Both were among IBM's largest and most sophisticated customers. Most of my time at Landmandsbanken was spent developing ideas to improve their bond management systems, including computerizing the whole list, calculating effective interest rates properly, before and after tax, and generally making it into a more user-friendly product. They got a head start on other banks in that area and dominated it for several years.

My first exposure to the currency market was when I was approached by the head of Landmandsbanken's foreign currency operations about a system he had heard about for switching currencies, developed by an IBMer in Germany. They sent me down to West Berlin to check it out. It used a quite sophisticated OR technique called "dynamic programming" to find the optimal "route" to switch from any currency to any other, given a matrix of exchange rates. But like many ideas that sound attractive at first glance, the system could never work in the real world. In those days you did not *have* instantaneous rates available. You had a bunch of telex machines chattering in the background and reams of paper tape all over the floor. By the time you made a calculation, the rates would have changed. So I advised that they not waste their time on it, and instead invest in a real-time electronic exchange rate system. Conditions in the "arbitrage" room were incredibly primitive those days compared to now. Those were the days of Bretton Woods, the dollar on the Gold Standard, and "fixed rates" that actually were not fixed at all, but operated within a very narrow band.

Eventually, I was ready to break the news to IBM, and went to tell the CEO. He took it very well and suggested we have a lunch of Eggs Benedict at the Imperial Hotel, which was right beside the IBM headquarters. Now, you have to understand that Eggs Benedict at the

Imperial was the highest honor he could bestow on anyone, whether his biggest client or Thomas Watson himself. He simply loved it (a single poached egg on toast with a touch of spinach) and expected naturally that everyone else did as well. When you ate with this particular CEO, you knew what you were going to get, nothing less, and perhaps more important, nothing more!

Of course he knew that we were going to be in a position to influence our clients' choices of computer equipment, so he wanted to have a good relationship. "As a matter of fact," he said, "by developing new application areas for computers, you and Peter may well be more valuable to IBM outside than inside," and he smiled as only a man who is sitting on 65% of the market can smile.

After I had been in Denmark about three months, in the Fall of 1964, Peter invited me over for afternoon coffee one Sunday to meet a friend, Hildur, "who likes to meet interesting people." Hildur, it turned out, was herself a very interesting person. She was 22 years old, very attractive, very outgoing, and with no false airs about her. She was about halfway through law school, and had known Vita since they lived under the same roof in their earliest years. She had a kind of uninhibited exuberance about her that fascinated me. I recall as we all went for a walk, how she suddenly without warning bounded on ahead, wildly jumping, singing and dancing in the middle of the road. She was simply happy and liked to show it. She was very different from me. Where I was a businessman interested in international finance, she was a grass roots activist with Marxist sympathies. Where I was stable, with very steady emotions, and not easily ruffled, she was wildly fluctuating. She was very much of her own mind, though, and not about to take a back seat to anybody. I always hoped to have a relationship that was based on equality. I liked strong women who could stand up for themselves and meet me on even terms. Unfortunately, I had seen very few and none of them had "clicked." Hildur was one, that was for sure. And she "clicked." Each of us seemed to sense a kind if completion of ourselves in the other. Each had something the other was missing. I think the die was cast that day, and we both knew it. A partnership was established for life.

The next few years were extremely challenging and exciting as Peter and I had the opportunity of tackling so many different problems at the top level of Danish industry in many different branches. In retrospect it was a unique occurrence due to the novelty of what we were doing and the fact that we had the whole field to ourselves.

In later years it would be much more difficult to get direct access to top level executives, as many others entered the fray, increasing the competition and shifting the goal posts. Besides which, there is a limit to how long you can go on dealing constantly with problems that have never been tackled before. There is also a limit to how many you can handle at once. Nevertheless, for quite a while, it was a fast track with never a dull moment.

In the midst of our hectic time building up the business, something happened that changed forever my approach to investment. When I was in the States, I did my Ph.D. on investment strategies in the stock market using options. I was used to following the stock market, and had made a few small investments while at University. So, soon after arriving in Denmark, I decided to take a look at the local stock market. I was single, earning a good income, my expenses were very low, and there was no withholding tax on income at the time, so I was building up some liquidity that I thought I could just as well put to use in the stock market.

My research had established that Palle Palsby was not only the largest broker in town, he was chairman of the Stock Exchange and vice-mayor of a suburb of Copenhagen—clearly a pillar of the establishment. In addition, he had his name on the only Danish stock index, the Palsby Index, published daily in all the newspapers—a clever public relations touch, I thought. So I met with Per Palsby, the son of the owner, who appeared to be about my age—I was twenty-six at the time. We quickly established that he was familiar with the kinds of transactions I wanted to do, and I came away in no doubt that this was the best place to do my business.

Over the next three years or so, I did a fair amount of business with Palsby & Co., almost always with Per. Only once did I meet Palsby senior, and only very briefly. From the start I made it clear with Per that I would make the decisions, and he would come with recommendations and comments. He should take no offense if I disregarded his advice. In fact, I found rather quickly that his advice was quite bad. Indeed, I noticed that he was almost *always* wrong about the short term moves in the market—which was actually quite good in a perverse way, as long as I did the opposite of what he recommended. So this I did very often with quite good results. There is nothing worse than a broker that gets it wrong half the time—better one that gets it wrong all the time!

Perhaps I should have been suspicious. In any case, it was first much later, after the dust had settled, that it dawned on me that there may have been a method to his madness—i.e., he may have been doing on his personal account the opposite of what he was recommending to his clients. A handy way to get out of an unwanted position!

After a couple of years, we had built up a portfolio of good blue chip investments, all fully paid, amounting to about $60,000 in market value, and Peter and I between us had another $14,000 personally, a sizable sum for us in those days.

In January of 1968 articles began appearing in the newspapers about Palsby, suggesting that he was in some kind of trouble. By late January, it was rumored that he was about to resign as chairman of the Stock Exchange. I did not like it one bit. Peter and I agreed to pull out everything at the first opportunity, which—after checking my calendar, was the following Tuesday, January 31, first thing in the morning. Peter agreed.

January 31 was a special day in more than one way. It was the date of the expected birth of our first child. When I opened the newspaper that morning, I received the shock of my life. The headline read "Palsby Bankrupt." I went straight to our lawyer with Peter for a briefing on what it all meant. We were about to get a devastating lesson in some curious aspects of Danish law. My initial concern was for the cash on deposit, about $7000. The news was much worse. I had considered Palsby basically as a depot for our paper, taking care of the book-keeping, dividends, etc. All our stocks were deposited in a special box in our name, with no permission for him to touch them in any way. I assumed we could have them delivered. They were after all our property and fully paid for, not his. Not necessarily, said our lawyer. Under Danish law, all holdings are considered part of the *broker's* assets, also customer holdings. It might be possible to have them delivered at some point as a so-called "separatist" holding. But not until the whole mess was straightened out.

In the weeks that followed, the picture of what had transpired began to crystallize. Apparently, Palsby got been speculating personal-ly in very large amounts, particularly in SAS, and got it very wrong. In desperation, he stole some of his customers' shares, sold them, and used the proceeds to cover his personal losses. Some customers were "luckier" than others. We were the absolutely "unluckiest." Every single one of our shares had been stolen. Those who had some shares left in their boxes got them eventually after about three years. As it turned out, if I had gone to Palsby on Monday and demanded our shares, I probably would have got them immediately—from somebody else's box. He was shuffling them around all the time apparently in order to keep afloat. It seemed obvious to me that he had favored some of his customers—probably his personal friends. We were a complete unknown to him, so he had no compunctions about cleaning us out completely.

A few weeks after the event, our lawyer hit us with another shock. It is not at all certain, he explained, that you can get a tax deduction for the loss. He explained that in Denmark, there is no deduction for losses of "wealth" when the wealth is stolen. If the shares had been sold for, say, one dollar, that loss would be deductible. But technically speaking, they were not sold, they were stolen. I was dumbfounded by this distinction.

There was, however, a deduction for working capital, if lost in this way. The problem was whether the tax authorities would accept our holdings of cash and shares at Palsby as "working capital," or claim it was "wealth," in which case the loss would not be deductible. He and our auditor advised us to proceed on the assumption that the working capital argument would prevail. The question was quite vital. If we knew for sure that the loss would not be deductible, we would be best off to liquidate the company and let the tax department share our loss. That way we could at least limit our loss to 100% of our net worth, and start from scratch with a new company. In the event, we decided to continue. After three years we finally got a tax ruling on this issue—no deduction allowable! We were all quite shaken. As a result, for some years we were effectively paying over one hundred percent of our running profit in taxes and were severely squeezed on liquidity in an undercapitalized company.

It is a sobering experience to lose over 100% of your net worth, and not without consequence. There would go over 25 years before I would ever buy another stock. I never dealt with any broker again. I became the world's most conservative investor. My only personal investments, besides my home and summer cottage, would be safe government and credit union bonds, even in my pension plan, all on deposit at the largest, safest bank available.

Fortunately for us, business was booming when Palsby failed, so we were able to continue on as if nothing had happened, with just a lot less in the bank to fall back on. The next few years were a time of new challenges in different branches every week.

These included optimizing the Danish Dairy Association's production mix for the domestic and foreign markets; production planning at a major instrument manufacturer; developing marketing strategies for an insurance company; simulating new schedules for the Copenhagen rapid transit system; optimal bidding strategies for tobacco; analyzing long term cash flow for a pension fund; developing optimal routing strategies for a major shipping company; optimal routing for a truck fleet, and much more, all at a breathtaking pace where the same problem was never seen twice.

One idea in 1969 which was good, but too early, was to market what was later to be known as a "spread sheet" which would allow even small firms to make realistic projections of their financial statements under various assumptions, using a computer terminal in their own offices. Decentralized terminals were beginning to revolutionize the way people did development work because they separated the user from dependence on the EDP Department, which in many large companies had developed into a monster of centralized, arrogant rigidity that choked off innovation and delayed many projects interminably. We anticipated that a simple accounts simulation package that could be quickly tailored to individual needs should be widely attractive—especially in cooperation with a far-sighted accounting firm with a captive client base. But events would later show that we were about ten years too early with the spread sheet concept, which first took off in a big way with the introduction of the personal computer in the late seventies.

Looking back from the vantage point of the year 2000, I was out of step with my contemporaries in more ways than one at the time. While part of the so-called "1968 generation" ("Don't trust anybody over thirty"), Hildur and I were more concerned with establishing our family, buying our first house, and for myself, building my business, than with making a revolution—especially a Marxist one.

The trendy Marxist thinking of the sixties left me—but not Hildur, cold, which created some minor clashes with some of our friends, who regarded me with some suspicion as a capitalist traitor. I felt Marxism was being misused by its proponents in Cuba and the Soviet empire in just another variation on the classical elitist power game that has plagued the common man throughout history.

In truth, I was not very enthusiastic about capitalism either—having personally experienced the downside when I lived in a black ghetto for two years in Cleveland, Ohio. Capitalism too, is a power game, albeit with different rules, and different winners and losers. It is cynical and without vision, but at least it is democratic. Actually, I thought the Danish "mixed economy" was a reasonable compromise between the two systems—taking some of the best parts of each system while avoiding the worst parts.

I was personally more interested in quite another subject entirely at the time, influenced greatly by Rachel Carson's "Silent Spring" on the pesticide threat. She warned that we were poisoning ourselves and heading for major disaster within twenty or thirty years—the typical lead time for many of these chemicals to enter the food chain. But she was talking to a deaf audience that was more concerned with other things and didn't seem to care about the environment.

Indeed, it is incredible that in the year 2000, chemicals like atrazin that were warned against 30 years earlier are still allowed into our drinking water in Western Europe. And when these pesticides are finally banned in the West one by one by an indignant public, they are simply exported to Third World countries that are less strict about the environment. That is one of the uglier sides of capitalism. And the communist states, as we saw after the Berlin wall came down, were even worse on the environment than the West.

Another area where Hildur and I were on a different wavelength than most of our contemporaries was in the way we wanted to live. We were both uninspired by the idea of a traditional suburban home in splendid isolation. Our wish was to establish a relationship with a few friends with small children, no fences, open doors, and some joint facilities, but with each family having its own home for privacy when required—a concept that in time came to be known as "cohousing."

When I look back now at some of the consulting jobs we did then, I cringe a little at how limited our vision was at the time, and how we helped to nudge development in the wrong direction without even realizing what we were doing. An example of this was the project for the Danish Slaughterhouse Association. Our job was to help them produce a twenty-year plan that could satisfy a very diverse assortment of slaughterhouse owners. It was an immense political task because everyone knew there were too many slaughterhouses, but no one wanted to be shut down. Some of the owners were building big, modern slaughterhouses in order to enhance their chances of survival, causing both dissension and overcapacity.

To make a long story short, Peter and I proposed an "ideal" approach which ignored the existing slaughterhouses and found the number and locations that would optimize the total cost of transportation (minimum with many slaughterhouses) and production costs (minimum with a few large slaughterhouses) assuming they were built from scratch with projected new technology. The solution was very innovative and elegant, and subsequently the subject of a number of articles in the literature due to its generality. The solution suggested an optimal number of only about 7-10 (the exact number not being critical) slaughterhouses as opposed to the seventy then in existence. This went down well with everybody as it indicated substantial savings for the Association, and provided an objective basis on which to go ahead politically. Indeed, over the next twenty years, the plan was carried out pretty much along the general lines indicated in 1968.

A classical successful case study, right? Yes and no! The most interesting part of this story is what we didn't include in the model—the *social costs*. When you close down 60 slaughterhouses and an even greater number of dairies (the same basic restructuring was applied to the dairy industry), you destroy the very infrastructure in the many small towns where they are a major source of employment. You destroy not only all those jobs, but many others in support industries and service industries as well, like the local grocery store.

The cost of progress? Perhaps. Although one should include in any analysis the indirect costs to the rest of society of all the disruption caused by such private sector restructuring. And we should define what we mean by "progress." Are ghost towns really what we want? What about the *quality* of life—the unquantifiable part? My point is that in 1968 *no one even asked this kind of question.* Come to think of it, in 2000 they still don't.

2

Environmental Crisis

By early 1972 I had enough extra time and energy to begin to expand my horizons and think about things other than my business and family life.

As far back as my early high school days, I had been fascinated with the way the world had developed in the past, and why, and I had thought a great deal about the challenges that would be faced by my generation. I enjoyed reading history in my spare time. HG Wells, Arnold Toynbee, and Will Durant were among my favorites. The public debate in Canada in the 1950s on the population explosion—how it was doubling every 35 years, made a lasting impression on me. That meant a quadrupling in my lifetime! I just couldn't imagine in my wildest fantasy how we were going to deal with that. Nobody else seemed to know either. A few years later, when I was working on a term paper at University, I again delved into that same topic and continued to see it as the major challenge in the coming years, but now in a more nuanced scenario tempered by other factors, such as technological unemployment, computerization, economic growth, centralization of government, and the survival of democracy.

So it was with this background that I read three very significant books in 1972 which were to have a lifelong effect on my thinking. The first was Barry Commoner's "The Closing Circle."[1] It was a shocker. Commoner—a highly respected American ecologist, had analyzed the incredible increase in pollution which had occurred in the United States over the 25 years since the war. Our air, water, and soil was getting filled with nitrous oxide, lead tetraethyl, mercury, phosphates, pesticides, synthetic fertilizer nitrates, plastics, radioactive waste, and much more to the tune of several hundred percent more than prewar levels. He pointed out that the increases were far, far beyond what was explainable by increases in population and consumption. Rather, it was the shift in the *method* of production that was the explanation. We were moving away from natural products that were biologically degradable, into synthetic products that were often non-degradable, and gradually poisoning ourselves in the process.

And why had this occurred? Superficially because the new production methods were cheaper. But, as Commoner pointed out, this was an illusion. They only appear cheaper because the indirect costs of maintaining the environment are not included. The latter costs are passed on to the general taxpayers and the next generation. In effect, commercial companies were using the environment as a dumping ground without being charged for it. It was profitable for them, but disastrous for society as a whole. Commoner estimated the clean-up costs at $40 billion for 25 years—about 3% of the GNP, a staggering number.

A second major point of Commoner was our erroneous natural resource accounting. Traditional production costs take into account only the costs of extraction of resources from the Earth, but do not include any depreciation of the resources. Such an approach makes sense only if one has unlimited resources. In all other cases, we underestimate the true cost. In effect we pass the cost on to future generations who will have to do without.

I was deeply shaken by Commoner's analysis, and quite convinced that he had made a startling discovery that would have wide-reaching consequences for the global economy and attract great interest. (How little did I know in my naiveté.) I did a review for Denmark's leading financial daily, a big two-page spread, and tried in general to stir up a debate. But to little avail. To my great surprise, no one seemed very concerned at all, not even the left wing politicians, who couldn't see what the environment had to do with Marxism.

It was clear to me that to shift production methods back where they belonged, it was necessary to include the environmental costs in the costs of production, for example, via a differential VAT, and feed the revenues into a special clean-up fund. Unfortunately, there was very little hard data on which to base such taxes, as ecology is a very complex affair, and everything is interrelated. A tremendous amount of research was needed as well as international cooperation.

I decided to initiate a research project to tackle the problem and applied on behalf of OAC to the Danish Research Council for a small grant of about $3000—just enough to cover our out-of-pocket salary costs—for a first-phase feasibility study just to define the scope of the problem and develop a proposal to carry out a comprehensive study. We had an excellent team of economists and engineers who were ideal for such a task. Though little known outside the field of economics, there was in fact an extensive literature on so-called "externalities"—the social costs that were normally omitted from economic models—going back to pre-war times.

I was soon in for a surprise. The Research Council had no idea what I was talking about, and could not see why one should spend money on such an untopical idea. We corresponded back and forth for six months until we had used up our entire budget just trying to convince them of the need to do a feasibility study. Finally I gave up, and went on to other things. That was my first and last experience of trying to work with the public research sector. Apparently it was almost unheard of for them to give research funds to a private firm for fear that there might be some profit element in it. And we thought we were doing society a favor by offering to put our think tank onto an important problem on a non-profit basis. That was a depressing experience.

In the meantime, the second book came out, "The Limits to Growth," by Dennis Meadows and his research team.[2] It was a popular version of a previous, more technical book I had read, "World Dynamics," by Jay Forrester of MIT, that came out in 1971, sponsored by the Club of Rome.[3] Forrester, a leading American operations researcher, had for many years pioneered development of the "systems dynamics" technique used by Meadows. This technique allows scenario simulation of complex systems having many interactions. In modern language, it was "non-linear," and thus capable of describing complex systems much more realistically than traditional "linear" models. I was familiar with Forrester's methods from my educational training, though I had never had occasion to use them in the practical consulting world, but was immediately struck by the appropriateness of his methodology to a modeling of major global trends. It was a stroke of genius—one of those very rare cases where a relatively simple model describes the real essence of a complex problem.

The essence of the Forrester/Meadows model was to challenge the greatest of all sacred cows in the twentieth century—economic growth as the elixir to solve all problems—and show that it was only a question of time until global growth becomes reversed by one or more interdependent factors—population growth, industrial pollution, resource usage, and food production—all of which have practical upper limits in a finite world. The model showed that whatever assumptions we put in, no matter how optimistic, one of these factors will sooner or later become limiting—and most likely in a time horizon of 50-100 years. In most scenarios, the end of growth comes with a total breakdown and collapse of global society.

I was greatly impressed by Meadow's work and felt it deserved broad dissemination, so I did an essay for a major Danish newspaper on the subject and arranged a public debate within the context of the Danish OR Society.

The following months saw a broad debate on the subject internationally. Most of the comments were critical, in particular from traditional economists, who did not like to see their turf threatened by outsiders. Some took issue with the accuracy of the data, creating a lot of doubt in the public mind. Others pointed out that using average global figures leads to erroneous results, and suggested that a more detailed regional model was necessary before any conclusions could be drawn. In fact, even very wide variations in the data had little effect on the general conclusions, but the damage was done.

I felt that a regional model would be so complicated that it would not have anywhere near the same pedagogical impact on the general public or politicians. This indeed turned out to be the case subsequently. Here we had a classical case of trying to find the right balance between a simple but essentially correct model that gets a powerful message across, and a detailed, more accurate model that is almost as difficult to understand as the original problem, and thus has no persuasive power.

The Limits to Growth model was eventually sunk by the growth economists, and a very important piece of research was buried without having any noticeable effect on policy. The economic growth syndrome was apparently too entrenched to dislodge—even on the political left.

Which leads me to the third book, one which some observers have nominated as the most important book of the twentieth century. Normally, a book on the history of science is for a limited audience and not the subject of wide debate. However, Thomas Kuhn's "The Structure of Scientific Revolutions" was an exception.[4] Kuhn, an American physicist, studied the historical development of science, and showed that the usual schoolbook presentation of science as a linear development of small, steady steps, was quite wrong. On the contrary, a more correct model would describe occasional quantum leaps, followed by long periods of "microscience," where small steps are taken within the new framework. Examples of quantum leaps would be the revolutionary works of Copernicus, Galileo, and Newton.

Characteristic for each quantum leap was a "paradigm shift"— Kuhn's catchy buzzword that was to become a part of our vocabulary in the late twentieth century. A paradigm shift is basically a radically new way of looking at an old problem that explains what is happening using a new point of viewing. Such a shift occurs very rarely, as we tend to be very fixed in the concepts and models we use. But then a crisis occurs. The old approach can no longer explain what is being observed. The old solutions no longer work.

Kuhn gives many examples of how even the best scientists of each age had great difficulty in accepting the revolutionary ideas of their younger colleagues. What starts as a model often ends as a belief system with religious overtones. It is not to be challenged.

The dominating paradigm in science is important because it permeates every aspect of society. It is not a technical detail of interest only to universities and research labs. For example, the dominating paradigm of this time in Western society is the Newtonian, mechanistic model which emphasizes reductionism and separatism, the separation of mind and matter, and postulates the existence of an objective universe outside of us. This has been a very successful paradigm in that it has been the driving force in bringing about the tremendous advances in our material well-being over the last three centuries. It is no coincidence that Western society is materialistic, consumption-oriented, and spiritually barren. These are all direct consequences of the Newtonian paradigm. The great majority of our citizens take these values as obvious and natural, but in the larger picture of civilizations, they are not. They are quite subjective. Many other types of society are possible.

Ironically, many of the basic tenets of the mechanical Newtonian world have already being shown to be incorrect by modern quantum theory—in particular the version known as the "Copenhagen School" developed by Niels Bohr and his followers. But these newer concepts have not yet had societal consequences. Their importance has not yet been recognized by the mainstream. We are in the middle of that process of change right now. It will take many years to complete. The most important of the differences from Newtonianism is the evidence that we cannot separate the observer from the observed. We know now that all things are interconnected, but in ways that we do not yet understand.

At some time in the future, when the history of our time is rewritten (as it always is from the perspective of the new age), I would not be surprised to see Niels Bohr cast in the role of the scientist who, more than anyone else, instigated the new paradigm of the twenty-first century—a paradigm of synthesis and holism that is still being formulated.

And this brings me back to 1972 and why I felt that this book with its new concept—the paradigm shift—was so important. It now became clear to me that what we were observing in the environmental crisis, in the population explosion, in the contrast between the absurdly rich of the West and the Third World elites on the one hand, and the poverty stricken homeless of the West and the starving poor of the Third World on the other—was a direct consequence of the very effective mechanical paradigm running its course. One could say that the seeds of its destruction were built into its very success.

In essence I saw the current crisis as a problem of scale more than anything else. The strategy of exploiting natural resources for the benefit of Mankind using reductionist science was quite appropriate when the population was relatively small and the environmental impact was limited, but became disastrous when continued on a fully populated planet with an advanced technology. It would have been absurd to introduce environmental protection in the early days of the industrial revolution. However today, the population is enormous. There are no new frontiers to move into like in the good old days. We have discovered that we live on a finite planet. Furthermore, modern technology is massively impacting the environment. A classical example (which came later but was entirely predictable in principle) is the Farrow Islands tragedy of the 1990s, where the world's most efficient shipping fleet was so technologically advanced in the "old paradigm" sense that it destroyed the very basis upon which it existed—the fish in the sea. The "new paradigm" slammed home the point that things do hang together in a holistic, finite world.

What we needed more than anything else was a paradigm shift away from the mechanistic way of thinking. Over the next few months I thought very deeply about the future of the planet, and the mechanisms that determine our destiny, mostly just to clarify my own thinking. On the whole, I was very pessimistic about the future based on the generally indifferent reactions to Commoner's and Meadow's books from politicians and others, and the realization that a paradigm shift to holistic thinking was a long way off. There was no real attempt to discuss alternative strategies, but lots of excuses for why we should not or could not do anything.

My general conclusion was that a voluntary braking of growth was probably politically impossible under current circumstances—not least due to the pressures from the Third World, who could only be pacified in the current world order as long as they had hope of a small piece of an ever increasing economic pie. Indeed, the same could be said about the less advantaged sectors of the industrialized countries. If the pie stopped growing, the powers-that-be were in for very big trouble from below. It will happen sooner or later. Denying that growth will ever stop is abdication of responsibility. But that is apparently what the electorate wants to hear, and what our politicians have to offer. So in a way, we get what we deserve. We are like the passengers on the "unsink-able" Titanic sailing into a sea of icebergs while dancing on the deck.

I felt that the introduction of the costs of environmental mainte-nance into market prices via product taxes and a differential VAT (Value Added Tax) was the way to take back control of industrial develop-ment. There was a need to integrate the Western economies with Third World economies rather than sending them hypocritical foreign aid that was nothing but a disguised discount on sales of Western industrial products, which were often the last thing they needed. I felt that only a complete change of mentality could bring about real action, a shift to a new concept of "inner growth" and an emphasis upon quality of life rather than consumption. I could see nothing on the horizon that was likely to lead to such a shift, and became in fact quite pessimistic about the future.

There would go almost ten years before I got my optimism back, and then only after a most unusual spiritual experience, which I will return to later.

3

Cohousing

It was around the time of our number two son's birth in 1969 that we started thinking about establishing a cohousing project. Hildur in particular was not keen on the idea of bringing up children in an isolated house in the suburbs, even less so in the city. She wanted "community," a network of friends and family that could give each other mutual support. This is the way human settlements existed for thousands of years, and still did in many parts of the world. But in the modern industrial state, with its separation of work and home, the traditional extended family was fragmenting, and rapidly becoming a thing of the past. More and more tasks were being taken over by institutions, from nurseries to old-age homes. While this development was well-intended, and to some extent a necessary corollary of industrialization, it was creating many unanticipated problems.

A new phenomenon was appearing—virtual isolation. Not physical isolation, but psychological isolation. The housewife in the suburbs alone with her children. The family in the new cement high-rise apartments who had little or no contact with others in the same block. Grandparents conveniently put away in special homes without contact with their families. The women's movement, with the resulting two-income family was not only a question of equality of the sexes, but was to some extent also a reaction to the problem of women's isolation. A job could create the human contact that was missing in virtual isolation, besides the obvious economic advantages. But there was a price to be paid, namely less contact with one's children, particularly in the very formative pre-school age, where they often had much more contact with the nursery school personnel than with their parents. We were both concerned about the possible effect on our children of too much institutional upbringing. Hildur was not happy having to choose between virtual isolation with two small children and a career that would separate her from the children in their most formative period. In the event, she felt the children were most important, and gave up her potential legal career after just one year. This was the background for us looking for a third way—cohousing.

A related development of the late sixties in Denmark was the "collective," often confused with cohousing, but really quite different. A collective was normally a single house in which several people were living, some single, some couples. Each would typically have his or her own bedroom, while the kitchen, living room, and dining room were common. A collective was not what we wanted. In our opinion, there was too little privacy, and too much forced contact with other people. Collectives had a very high turnover rate for this reason, and were appropriate mostly for young single people for a limited period of their lives.

Our cohousing vision was that each family would have its own home, but would share some common facilities, such as a meeting and party room, a washing and drying room, a common office space, a workshop, a garden shed, a chicken coop, etc. There would be no fences or other artificial divisions between the homes. Members, particularly the children, would be welcome in each others' homes without formalities, but with due respect for privacy. This would create the feeling of togetherness and openness that is lacking in the typical neighborhood, while preserving privacy when that is what is wanted. Many local neighborhoods used to function like this in the 1940s and 1950s. I was brought up in one myself. But things had changed, and those neighborhoods were becoming harder and harder to find. No cohousings existed at the time, so we would have to start from scratch.

One of the advantages of creating our own cohousing was that we could choose the people we would be living with, in a so-called "intentional community." This was much better than simply moving into an attractive neighborhood and taking your chances. So we gradually became part of a small circle of young couples that shared the vision. Some had small children, some not. We began looking for an appropriate place, but this turned out to be far more difficult than we had imagined.

Other people were thinking along similar lines in the 1960s. One of the first projects was in the Copenhagen suburb Farum, with thirty-three units in a new development. We considered it, but our group wanted something smaller, and if possible, north of Copenhagen. Many years later, the architect of that project, Jan Gudmand-Høyer, became something of a guru in the American cohousing movement, which took off in a big way in the early 1990s, based largely on the successful Danish model.

It took about three years and many outings before we seriously considered Daphne Bray's riding school as a possibility. We became neighbors in 1968 just before Christmas when we moved in next door. We had hardly lived there two days when a commotion prompted us to look over the stake fence and observe her unique form of Christmas celebration with a dozen horses dancing around a Christmas tree in the middle of the courtyard of the three-winged farmhouse, while dozens of young girls rode and sang and pulled horses every which way. Through a massive hole in the straw roof of the stables descended a fully costumed Santa Claus with gifts for all—the horses, that is—half a loaf of rye bread to each! The girls were ecstatic.

At one point, we caught her attention and she came over to welcome us: "Won't you join me for a glass of sherry?" she asked sweetly in Oxford English. "You can put the boy in one of the stalls. That's what I used to do with my girls," she laughed. She could speak enough Danish to get by, but generally spoke English to everyone. Thus began the sherry ritual that we would come to repeat many times over the next four years whenever Daphne had something she wanted to talk about.

Daphne was the 50-something widow of a British diplomat who had died many years before in a plane crash. She decided to stay on in Denmark and raise her four girls alone, earning her living from this riding school where she had been since the early fifties. She lived alone now, and ponies were her life.

And dogs, I thought, as we were ushered into her living room. Five golden retrievers sat around on the living room chairs and sofas, making themselves at home as if to join us in drinks. Daphne took it all in stride as the most natural thing in the world. The house seemed very run down and in great need of maintenance. The furnishings were old and tarnished. But when I heard she had 37 ponies and no help, I could see she didn't have time for much else. She was also quick to apologize and went into a routine that we were to hear many times, complaining of how expensive everything was, and how difficult it was making ends meet. The suggestion that she consider selling a few horses and operating at a more modest level brought a howl of protest— they were her "friends" and couldn't be sold!

At one point, as we sipped our sherry, I heard a strange clunking sound in the hall, and then suddenly a horse poked its head into the living room as if to say hello. I said to Daphne, slightly shocked by the sight: "Surely you don't allow your ponies into the house?"

"Oh, no!" said Daphne indignantly, "only this one!" and broke into a big smile as she fed it a biscuit.

As time went on, we got to know Daphne better and became close friends. She was a proper English lady—rather out of place here perhaps—but doing a tremendous job with the 11 to 15 year-old girls in the neighborhood, who learned to take responsibility and do a hard day's work. Some almost seemed to live there. And it was a lot of work mucking out, feeding, and keeping clean all those ponies. Daphne had a real sense of celebration, and arranged all kinds of birthday parties, jumping competitions and beauty contests where the ponies showed up with braided tails and ribbons on their foreheads in a great display of pomp.

It was hard on Daphne, though, and I sometimes wondered how long she could keep it up. One day, she showed up with a very nasty cut on her arm, and explained that she had been thrown off her horse carriage and run over by one of the wheels. She just got on with the work with no complaints.

There were lighter moments too. Like the time I wandered over and found her mucking out in a nice dress. What was that all about? "Oh," she said, with a touch of pride, "I've just come from lunch with two Queens—Margrethe and Ingrid."

One day she talked wearily about maybe selling the place and retiring to a more leisurely life with her favorite horses, so I mentioned to our little group the possibility of a cohousing at this site. Daphne's place had several attractions, as there were two current residences and four building lots, right beside our place, which included an extra lot. The others took a look and liked the idea.

But Daphne was difficult to nail down. On several occasions, I broached the subject, but she was constantly wavering and uncertain, and usually changed the subject before reaching any conclusion. I was slightly mystified. She wouldn't spend money on a lawyer or a real estate agent so it was difficult to make any progress. Besides, I didn't want to push her into something she would regret. One day, after hearing more complaints about meeting bills, I asked her why she didn't just borrow some money on her property. She had only mortgaged it for $2000 and it was worth at least $100,000. But she would not do it on principle, nor would she take advice from anybody, including me.

One day, after speaking with the others, my friend John and I visited her and put forward on behalf of the group a concrete proposal for $140,000 with normal down payment and mortgage conditions. She had finally engaged a real estate agent, and our offer was very close to her asking price. Nevertheless, she was evasive, and instead of giving a straight answer, hemmed and hawed endlessly. It was all very frustrating. We were getting nowhere. Then John got a brilliant idea.

"Daphne," he said, with a devious glint in his eye, "How would you like us to pay you in hard cash? Bills only. They would make a pile roughly this high," and he held his hand well above the table. I calculated quickly in my head, and added, "It would be about $100,000. Cash on the table."

Daphne suddenly sat up straight in her chair as if someone had poked her in the back, and looked back and forth at us with wide eyes: "Really? Are you serious? Gentlemen, let us have a glass of sherry," she said, smiling, and headed resolutely for the liquor cabinet. John knew and I knew that it didn't make a bit of difference to us how we paid. We could take out a loan if she wanted cash. But I was stymied. I whispered to John: "How did you figure *that* out?"

"Her eyes," said John. "Every time you mention the word 'mortgage,' her eyes glaze over. She won't admit that she doesn't have the foggiest notion how a mortgage works."

And so it came about that we all got together on September 30, 1972, at Daphne's to sign a sales agreement. Everything seemed to be in place for the closing as midnight approached. Per, our legal advisor as well as group member, gave the papers to Daphne to sign.

She put on a serious face and exclaimed: "I am not going to pay that incompetent real estate agent, who did nothing for me, but insists on his fee. You will have to pay him or there is no deal."

We looked around at each other, a little annoyed. It was her agent, not ours. Rather bold of her, we thought. We shrugged. A little out of the ordinary, but then what is ordinary about Daphne Bray? OK, we said, a little disgruntled, if that is what it takes to get this over with.

Feeling the taste of victory, Daphne then reached into her pocket, pulled out a slip of paper, and waved it at us: "Plus my dentist's bill for 2000 kr."

Per was falling off his chair. I guess he'd never negotiated like this before. "That is quite out of order," he pointed out. "We had agreed on the price."

"Then there is no deal," said Daphne, and stood up indignantly, as our eyes collectively rolled across the ceiling. I thought, my God, she is a good negotiator. She has us by the short hairs and knows it. We looked around at each other shaking our heads in wonder at this performance, collectively sighed and gave in. OK. We eat the dentist's bill. And so the deal was done, and we all had a glass of sherry. Cohousing project "Højtofte" would be a reality as of January 1, 1973.

Daphne did not take long to celebrate. Shortly after she got her cash she drove up the long driveway to show off her new Mercedes convertible, of somewhat vintage quality, wearing her favorite broad-brimmed straw hat—and with all five golden retrievers seated around her in front and back—with the biggest smile I had ever seen. She walked over to my place and asked me for some investment advice: "Ross, what do you think I should do with all this money that I have now?"

"Well," I said, smiling, "The safest thing would be to buy some mortgage bonds. I'd be glad to help you pick out some. If you want to go for a higher return you might consider a private second mortgage bond, for example on that house over there. I can recommend it," and I pointed to her former residence. I am not sure whether Daphne caught the irony, but from the squint in her eye and her long silence, I think she was beginning to get it.

In due course, Daphne moved to a rented place in the country, and true to her professed feelings, she would not sell her dearest "friends," but took about 15 of them with her, mostly the old and the sickly.

A very important aspect of living in the cohousing was the close-ness of the children—to each other, and to the adults. They all felt wel-come everywhere. And the parents all felt that they had a responsibil-ity and a special attachment to the many children. Everyone helped to bring up the others' children as well as their own. Everyone became a lot closer than you could ever imagine. Having several adult role mod-els is also a big advantage for growing children. They quickly learn that you don't necessarily have to be like your parents, that there are other possibilities. They learn that you have to behave very differently *this* place than you do *that* place, and that there are many different ways to resolve problems, and to pass the time. They form very realistic atti-tudes towards life in general. They become very robust, very well-rounded individuals.

One of the mainstays of the cohousing was the obligatory Wednesday evening meeting. Over the years this went through several phases. There were always practical problems to be dealt with—the chicken-feeding program, the common room cleaning program, plan-ning the next "work weekend," which was typically once every month or two in the early years, as the old buildings needed a lot of mainte-nance. And planning the program for future meetings. Sometimes guests were invited. There were times when we would invite a guest speaker to make a presentation, if someone had an interesting visitor. Other times one of the members would tell about a special experi-ence—say a trip to Nepal, or India.

Celebrations and fun were also given a prominent place in the cohousing. Everyone's birthday, children as well as adults, was normally celebrated with drinks at 5 o'clock. Round birthdays were often occasions to celebrate in real style, and Højtofte developed its own special tradition of putting on a tailor-made, side-splitting, special number for the guest-of-honor. Then there was the annual "open house" in June, where everybody invited a dozen or so guests, or the annual picnic in August, always to some place we hadn't been to before. Then there was the annual "English Christmas," which was initiated by John (from England) and myself in the mid-1970s to show the Danes how the English culture celebrated Christmas, with turkey, Waldorf salad, chestnut purée, mincemeat pie, and Christmas pudding. And with lots of games and puzzles for the children and the adults, and with all the traditional English Christmas carols. It was so popular that it continues to this day with the same original cast, even though we and John's family moved away several years ago. The children always looked forward to it with even greater anticipation than to the regular Christmas. All these things were what made life in the cohousing different from your typical neighborhood. They added an extra dimension of quality of life that is indescribable and irreplaceable.

Perhaps the greatest indication of the success of this experiment in living is that just about all the children—now in their twenties, say they would like to form a cohousing themselves when they are ready to have children. Only time will tell if they manage it. The hurdles are still quite considerable, even after all these years. There are, at last count, about 150 cohousings in Denmark, and somewhat more in the USA, where they are spreading rapidly.

4

Muktananda

In February, 1982, I attended a conference on Transpersonal Psychology in Bombay, my first trip to India. This rather unusual step for me had been prompted by a most unusual "power" experience I had had while doing a so-called "holotropic breathing" workshop with Stanislav Grof, the well-known Czechoslovakian psychiatrist, best known for his experiments with LSD, which had been banned by the early 1980s. I experienced feelings that I previously had not in my wildest imagination believed were possible. Grof was chairman of the Bombay conference and suggested I attend in order to get a better insight into my experience. It turned out to be the most significant event of my life to date, a watershed event that changed everything.

The conference itself was very invigorating and inspiring. For the first time in my life, I was meeting en masse people who saw the world through very different lenses than the great majority. There was no end to the revolutionary new thinking that abounded in all fields of endeavor. My strong feeling was that this group was on the leading edge of a very significant shift in human history, away from the narrow thinking of materialism and exploitation of nature and into something entirely new, which was still being defined. My intuition was that this group was laying the very foundation of a new culture. Besides Stan Grof there was Rupert Sheldrake, the English biologist with his "morphological field" theory. There was Karl Pribram, the American neurosurgeon, with his holographic brain model. There was Fritjof Capra, the Austrian physicist, linking ancient Taoist thought with modern physics. Then there was the ghost of the conference, Ilya Prigogine, the Belgian Nobel prize-winning chemist, who was not there personally, but whose revolutionary ideas about creating order out of chaos were the talk of the corridors. And then there were the hundreds of ordinary folks from all walks of life that were not at all ordinary, each with a fascinating story to tell.

But most of all, there was Swami Muktananda, a Siddha Yoga master and a main speaker at the conference, whom I had heard so much about before he even made his appearance. Most of the stories were first hand accounts of the strange, unbelievable reactions of people to "Shaktipat," the procedure whereby Muktananda awakened the latent "kundalini" energy at the base of the spine—reactions like cramps, visions, ecstasy, temporary physical and mental illness, uncontrollable body movements called "kriyas," involuntary yoga positions, hot and cold feelings, ants crawling up the spine, and much, much more. This was not idle talk, but serious accounts by professional people from all kinds of backgrounds, who had as much difficulty with understanding it as anyone else. But he was for real, with three hundred thousand followers world-wide.

In his talk, he explained the reactions as part of a cleansing process that he initiated, and which proceeded on an individual basis for each person as long as was necessary to rid the body of all blockages and sickness. The process could take years to complete, even a whole lifetime, leading eventually to the state of the higher self, our ultimate birthright. Kundalini awakened under his control was tailor-made to the individual so he or she did not get more than could be handled. Awakened in this way, he claimed it was not dangerous, as it could be if awakened spontaneously or through forced methods, such as certain types of breathing exercises. He was the latest in a line going back to the beginnings of time that had this special gift, which had previously been a secret ancient initiation. He explained that kundalini energy was not intended to create a passive state of well being, but to transform us on every level, including our worldly life. Kundalini is the secret of life, said Muktananda, the creative power of the universe known as the holy spirit in Christianity. In our present state, we identify ourselves with our bodies, but when the kundalini is awakened, we become aware of our true, divine nature. He concluded his talk with an invitation to the conference participants to visit his ashram at Ganeshpuri, about 60 miles north of Bombay. I was deeply moved by his talk and decided to follow his suggestion to visit his ashram for a few days after the conference.

But first, I was to experience one of the most remarkable days of my life, which I see now in retrospect as a part of the whole event that was unfolding. It was the last day of the conference. We had the afternoon off before taking the bus to Ganeshpuri next morning. And what an afternoon! I heard in the corridors that there was a possibility to meet two Indian "gurus" who were in Bombay that day, and hopped into a taxi with some Scandinavian friends with little idea of what was in store. The first stop was a visit with none other than Babaji—*the* Babaji of Haidakhan, spoken of by Yogananda in his well-known "Autobiography of a Yogi." Many people considered Babaji to be the most highly evolved person alive, and would give their right arms to meet him. His fame as a spiritual leader was unsurpassed, but he was inaccessible under normal circumstances, preferring the Himalayan mountains as his habitat. He very seldom came to Bombay. Nevertheless, the five of us had a short visit with him, receiving his blessings along with a number of Indians and a few others from the conference. One Indian told me it was the greatest moment of his life.

The second stop was, in its way, just as remarkable. The person we visited was a faith healer from Delhi named Sadachari, who also came to Bombay only once in a while. His function was very much like a Western doctor, but his methods were strictly Eastern. The remarkable thing about Sadachari was that he knew everything about us, who we were, and what each of us had written about ourselves on pieces of paper folded and cast into a silver urn. Most amazing of all, he literally materialized out of the thin air something for each of the five of us—either vibuthi (sacred sandalwood ash) or a broach of Buddha or Jesus, depending on what the person had written (vibuthi for me). Even the Indians who saw what happened were amazed and wanted to know who we were. He had never done that before apparently. I am not exaggerating. Each person who was there can verify what I am reporting: Danish anthropologist Annette Leleur, Danish journalist Bente Arendrup, and the Swedish medical doctor and TV personality Bengt Stern. I never got the name of the fifth person, a Finnish student of architecture. Clearly we were all shaken to the bone. Our Western materialistic scientific paradigm had been given a mortal blow. I was at a total loss to explain what was going on. But there is no doubt that what happened was authentic. This was my first personal "smoking gun" proof of the existence of paranormal phenomena that I had only read about. I was keener than ever to see Muktananda, who hopefully might provide a comprehensible answer to my mounting questions.

Ganeshpuri turned out to be a rather small and simple settlement of about two thousand inhabitants out in the country. The ashram, with its one thousand or so beds, was actually rather isolated a mile or so outside of town, and surrounded by farmland. The main temple, facing directly onto a dirt street, was a two-story yellow structure with an attractive facade of decorative windows, ornaments, and an archway leading into a small outdoor courtyard. Here everyone took off their shoes and placed them neatly on a rack or out of the way along the brick wall before entering the temple.

At the other end of the courtyard I checked in and found out where I was sleeping—a men's dormitory with about twenty to a room. We were told that we should make ourselves at home, and kindly note the rules of the ashram. At 3:00 p.m., Muktananda would hold 'darshan' for visitors. This was a twice daily ceremony where Muktananda would appear in the main hall and be available for about two hours for any and all who wished to have a word with him. The rest of the time he was elsewhere taking care of administrative matters, meditating, writing, and so on.

I noted the ashram rules and daily schedule, which were posted prominently in the courtyard. Strictly no smoking, drugs, or alcohol. Any offenders would be summarily evicted. No sexual contact, not even holding hands. Talk should be kept to a minimum and be quiet. An exception was the eating area where it was OK. This was a place of worship with an iron discipline. The daily schedule for residents included wake-up at 3:30 a.m. and lights out at 9:00 p.m. In between were regular times for chanting, working, eating, meditation, and a little free time for reading, etc. For new arrivals and guests, nothing was obligatory the first three or four days. But after that, one was expected to enter the routine and take on some job around the ashram. The cost was fifteen dollars per day for a cot and meals.

I kicked off my sandals and walked barefoot into the temple. It was like entering a magical world. The floors were of cool marble, the air thick with the sweet fragrance of sandalwood ash and burning incense. Most striking of all, though, was the sound of chanting which reverberated powerfully throughout the main hall as male and female voices alternated. It was an expansive, beautiful hall, sunken a few steps down from the entrance corridor. Dominating the immediate area was a statue of Muktananda's predecessor, Nityananda, standing amid a beautiful flower garden. To the left was an elevated platform with red and beige cushions spread about which I assumed was Muktananda's place. To the right of the statue was an archway which led to the gardens. The many plants and open structure gave a feeling of being very close to nature. The walls were beautifully and tastefully decorated. Further to the right was a large floor area where about two hundred people sat with their backs to me, women on the left, men on the right, chanting alternatively:

women: Hari Krishna,
      Hari Krishna,
      Krishna Krishna,
      Hari Hari

men: Hari Rama,
     Hari Rama,
     Rama Rama,
     Hari Hari

One of the residents mentioned that the ashram had just started a nonstop forty-eight hour chant. The idea was that people would come and go so that there was always roughly the same number chanting night and day. We were welcome to join in if we wished. The residents seemed to be of all ages, but with a preponderance of fairly young people. They seemed to be very pleasant as smiles came easily. They were simply but tastefully dressed in summer clothes, as it was quite warm.

The entire effect was electric, timeless, mystical, mesmerizing, powerful, unworldly. There was nothing to indicate that we were in the twentieth century.

I felt very much at home, and just drank in the atmosphere. I wandered into the garden. It was quite extensive and varied with many interlocking pathways. The flowers and bushes were beautiful and well kept. Here and there were various statues and busts of different sages, often colorfully painted. There were a number of benches where one could relax.

As I wandered I realized that the ashram was quite extensive with many buildings, including workshops, agricultural buildings, a western-style cafeteria, kitchen, and various offices besides the dormitories and main temple. Then I discovered the book shop, which had a quite extensive selection. I picked up a couple of Muktananda's books; there were about twenty to choose from.

At 3:00 p.m. it was time for darshan, where we all got in line to meet Muktananda. He took his place where I had suspected on the elevated platform. There was only time for a very short exchange. The woman in front of me had said something about the path that led her here. When she finished, I said that my path had been that of Western science. He seemed very alert and said:

"There are many paths. But there is no fundamental difference between East and West."

I said I could agree with that, and added that I liked very much the atmosphere of the temple and was looking forward to my stay.

After darshan, it was soon time for dinner. One could choose between the western-style cafeteria and the Indian food. I found a place in the large hall where the Indian food was served. Everyone sat on a bare cement floor in long rows. First came a "plate" in the form of about six giant, stiff leaves sewn together. Then came a pile of rice in the middle and an assortment of spicy vegetables forming a circle around the rice, a glass of water, and a little sauce. No knives or forks. Just dip your fingers in the rice, then in the vegetable of your choice, and get it into your mouth as best you can. The house rule was: take as much as you like as long as you eat everything.

Sitting cross-legged was a form of mild torture for my knees, so this was not quite my style. A nice touch though was the efficiency. On the way out everybody just folded the remains up in their leaves and threw them into a special container which would be emptied into the fields eventually as fertilizer. No plates or cutlery to wash. No tables and chairs to worry about. Neat! I took part in an evening prayer, said goodbye to a number of people from the conference and went to bed early. There wasn't much choice.

The next day was a relaxing treat. I slept well, not caring to get up in the middle of the night with the residents, then took my time wandering around the ashram. The continuous chanting created a strange unworldly feeling. I took part in it for a while. There was a tremendous surge of power each time the verse shifted from men to women and back again. The chanting seemed to develop in waves, first a number of quiet verses, then an increasing intensity for a while, followed by a tapering off. It seemed to have a life of its own, and be pulling along everyone with it. It was hypnotic, soothing. It was impossible to think of everyday problems, or even the world outside with that continual rhythm and the fragrant air and the beauty all around. I chatted briefly with various people here and there as I got a feel for the place. I read a little in the books I had picked up, and kept well away from the Indian-style dining room. My knees dictated that I would eat in the cafeteria from now on, even though the selection was rather limited.

But mostly I just let my thoughts wander as I digested all the new information from the conference. I began to think in terms of how to put together the ideas of Grof, Muktananda, Capra, Prigogine, Sheldrake, etc., and the materialisations of Sadachari into a single pattern that made sense internally without worrying about scientific beliefs for the moment. What kind of a world was evolving from all this? What kind of intelligence was behind it? What was the role of the individual?

What was the purpose? The meaning of it all? And how did it relate to my experience with Grof?

In the evening, after sundown, I wandered down the road to Ganeshpuri and back again. Along the road were some small shops—almost stands really—that sold trinkets and sundry small things. There were still a number of people about, mostly wearing long, flowing robes. A couple of hundred yards from the ashram, only a few lights here and there separated the dirt road from complete darkness. A rumbling in the dark turned out to be an oxen-drawn cart with wooden wheels that seemed to rise suddenly out of the dark road like a ghost from the past. It could easily have been like this two thousand years ago, I thought. Time seemed to stand still in this eerie atmosphere. My thoughts wandered idly as I approached the lighted-up area of the ashram again, looking up into a clear starlit sky.

Suddenly I felt a tingling sensation in my leg—very strong—a little like goose pimples but not the same. Then without warning, came a slight tremor in my body as if I were passing through an invisible barrier. Something seemed to go 'pop'—whoosh, whoosh. For just a second or two. Then I woke up. Pow! Just like that.

I looked around. Everyone seemed to be asleep, walking along the road as if in a dream. My first thought was: "My God, we have all been asleep. I must be the first to have woken up. What is going on? I had better wake up the others and find out." Then I thought "Who's in charge here? Who is running this dream? Where is the leader?" I felt almost like I was alone, abandoned on some foreign planet and was standing there among all these projections walking around in their dream and without contact with my people. "What am I supposed to do now?" I thought. I think I said aloud:

"OK. What's the game plan?" half expecting some kind of response from somewhere, some acknowledgment, some instructions. Nothing happened, except a few curious passers-by looked strangely at me. Then I thought: "There has got to be a control, a committee, something, somebody." I thought: "When I snap my fingers they will appear. We'll have a meeting. Find out what's going on." I snapped my fingers. Nothing happened.

I tried another approach. I'll count to three. When I count to three, everybody wake up. I counted to three, and shouted:

"OK. Wake up, everybody!"

Nothing happened, except a few more people looked at me like I was drunk or crazy. All of this happened within no more than one minute or so after the awakening. My next thought was: "Of course, they don't know they are asleep, and if I don't cool it, they are going to make trouble for me. No point in attracting attention. This whole thing may be much more complicated that I imagine." So I smiled at the Indians on the street, who were beginning to look a little concerned at my strange behavior, and walked into the ashram determined to keep a low profile and think through this whole weird situation from A to Z before I did anything, or talked to anybody.

The first thing I noticed was the change in my body. Everything felt perfect. I flexed my fingers. They seemed much thinner, more powerful, as if they had been swollen and clumsy before. It was the same with the rest of my body. As I walked it felt completely natural, rhythmic, beautiful, perfect—the way it should be, I thought! I had never imagined one could feel so perfect. I felt like I could do anything I wanted to physically. I couldn't get over this wonderful feeling, and ran my hands up and down my arms, my legs, my chest. It was unbelievable. It was as if, for the first time in my life, I really experienced myself completely naturally, completely at ease. I began to sense my true nature, and I liked it immensely.

There was no doubt whatsoever that this was a non-ordinary state. I have felt euphoria before. There was no comparison. This was not just a "peak experience." This was far more powerful. It was also far more exhilarating than a sexual orgasm, a constant high really. I could also feel my sexual energy like a powerhouse. It gave a fantastic feeling of strength.

One thing had been perfectly clear to me from the beginning, and I now returned to that thought. It was the same feeling as that time with Grof. The same power. Superman in spades I had called it. Exactly. The same icily clear feeling in mind and body. Only there was no anger, no aggression this time, only deep feelings of love and compassion. Nor did I lose any of the power this time. I recalled now the very instant of the breakthrough how the power surged through me and I seemed to grab it and control it. Unlike the first time, this time I had hold of it right from the start and felt in complete control now. There was no fall off of the power at all. I felt no need to use it as I had with Grof. I realized now that my reaction then had been wrong. So I just relaxed and relished the fantastic feeling while I surveyed the scene in the ashram.

Everyone seemed to be sort of floating by me as if they were sleepwalking. I felt as if I were observing their joint dream. There was no sparkle in their eyes. I felt strongly that they were projections from their real selves, just shadows of what they could be if they were fully awake. They all seemed so intent on going somewhere or doing something that was entirely irrelevant. It was as they were projections onto a cosmic film.

My thoughts turned to Muktananda and kundalini. Was that what I had experienced? The answer was far from clear. In favor of a kundalini interpretation was the fact that it had happened right here. But everything else seemed against this interpretation. I had by now been to several lectures, read a few books, and heard a lot of anecdotes about kundalini. Nowhere had I come across anything remotely similar to my experience. I experienced no colors, no feelings of ants crawling up my spine, no pains, no "kriyas," no feelings of energy rising, no heat, no mental disturbances. I had never felt better in my life. In fact this was the most real moment of my life. Completely awake for the first time. Then there was the fact that I had experienced the same feeling before with Grof. There was no Muktananda there. All in all, I concluded that if it hadn't happened right here, I would never even have thought of kundalini as a possible explanation.

There was however the feeling of super awareness that Muktananda mentions—all my senses were super sensitive—and the strong sexuality. Also I could identify with the feeling of witness consciousness that Muktananda writes about—where one observes oneself and everything else with cool detachment and no ego involvement. I felt very much like that. In summary, there was no clear-cut answer to the kundalini question.

I retired to my room and let my thoughts wander. There is no hurry, I thought. I have all the time in the world to work it out. All week and nothing else to do but work it out. But I couldn't sleep. My brain seemed to be operating at two or three times normal speed, and I just couldn't make it slow down.

A thought occurred to me. Was I experiencing a state of the future? Some kind of early warning?. Was I experiencing—as one of the first perhaps—how it was going to be for everyone later? Let's think in terms of biology and evolution. Think of a flower blossoming. Look at the Earth as a flower in the garden of the universe. How do you get it to evolve to where it can reach its full potential? Well, you would have to reach a certain level of maturity. You would probably need a critical mass in terms of people. You would probably need some form of global communication network. And you would probably need a certain level of technology that enabled you to operate on a large scale.

Maybe you would need some special form of energy as well, analogous to the sunshine in the Spring. The Aquarian Age? There could be a number of "triggers" that are beyond our comprehension at this time. Then you would have to have a plan, a vision, a blueprint for the flower. Finally, you would need people to carry it out. To do this, Man—or at least a portion of Mankind—would probably have to remove the Maya veil and wake up. Otherwise you would be more likely to destroy yourself than evolve to a higher level.

I thought of Prigogine. We are like individual molecules and we are being perturbed, on a global scale, by a technology that is too powerful for us to handle in the dream state. We will have to wake up soon. But perhaps we must come close to the brink in order to make the shift. It would be a delicate operation. Such is nature. Not at all certain of success. We might not make it.

I thought of the Gaia hypothesis recently put forward by the atmospheric chemist James Lovelock. Gaia was the Greek goddess for Mother Earth. The Earth, says Lovelock, is a living organism with its own self-regulating mechanisms. There is no way that the curious mixture of gasses in our atmosphere could have arisen or could persist by chance. It is just too far from chemical equilibrium. And amid all the apparent disorder, conditions favorable for life are somehow maintained in a very narrow range of temperature and composition.

And what are we doing today? We are tampering with Gaia on an unprecedented scale, destroying the rain forests, damaging the ozone layer, polluting limited sources of fresh water, tampering with the level of carbon dioxide in the atmosphere, poisoning our food with pesticides, using up limited oil sources in a few generations. Looking at the situation objectively, there can't be much time left. We must be very close to a make or break point.

I thought of the many prophecies of great catastrophes for the latter part of this century—the biblical prophecies, Nostradamus, Edgar Cayce and a myriad of other clairvoyants. Perhaps they received valid information, but misinterpreted it. Perhaps what we are experiencing is the blossoming of the flower Earth. Think of the tremendous change that occurs when a bud opens up. A clairvoyant molecule in a bud could only interpret the future as a catastrophe. Think of a clairvoyant caterpillar who gets a precognitive feeling of becoming a butterfly. Utter disaster! And what would the flower look like. Suppose everyone woke up right now and decided to make the Earth flower, what would it look like?

Man is part of nature, probably the highest level on this particular planet. Then the flower would have to be nothing less than Man's culture in its myriad forms, like a forest with ten thousand varieties of flowers—each one as unique, as beautiful, as worthy as the next. Some small, some large, some ancient, some modern, some rural, some urban. In every color of the rainbow. And with self-sufficient appropriate technology. To develop such a flower would mean rediscovering our roots, finding our cultural identities, creating new ones.

And what would be the mechanism to bring it about? Prigogine's work suggests an answer—self-organizing systems! Such a flower could never be designed from the top down, but only from the bottom up, by grass-roots local initiative. A decentralized explosion of energy with a global vision.

And what would be the life philosophy of this new society? Precisely what we have been talking about at the conference. A rejection of empty materialistic, egoistic modes of thinking, and an acceptance of a holistic, ecologically stable, more spiritual life. Not institutionalized religion with external gods that alienate the individual from his higher self, but a back-to-basics empowerment of the individual as the true source of divinity. God is within, as every great religious teacher has always said. The original and universal teachings must be rediscovered, the paraphernalia of false differences thrown out.

Is it utopia? Daydreaming? Unrealistic? Technically, organizationally, I didn't think so. Mainly it's a matter of priorities. But without the awakening, doubtful if it could be pulled off politically.

I decided to wander back to afternoon darshan and have a chat with Baba. As I walked along the footpath the faint music of the ashram, which I could see in the distance, floated across the foothills. The forty eight hour chant was over. Now it was a recording of Paul Horn's flute in the Taj Mahal. Beautiful, eerie music that made this whole scene seem unworldly.

Darshan was well underway when I arrived, as people sat around on the floor of the temple alone or in small groups and a few stood in line to see Baba. It was soon my turn. I outlined my vision of Gaia and the flowering Earth. Baba nodded approvingly in silence. The interpreter said it was very beautiful, and shed a few tears as he was very moved. Then Baba said just three words:

"Start with yourself."

The full story of that experience and my subsequent spiritual journey is recorded elsewhere.[1] But looking back now from the vantage point of eighteen years later, I can say that the on-site interpretation outlined above—written shortly after the experience, remains very close to my understanding today of what is happening to us globally. Similar interpretations have been put forward in the meantime quite independently by a number of persons from different parts of the world, in different, but fundamentally similar variants. Strange as it may seem to the vast majority of citizens of the planet, the reality of our existence is apparently very different from what we have been led to believe. However, until each of us experiences this on a personal level, this claim must necessarily be precisely that—a claim.

Nevertheless, more and more people are reaching conclusions similar to mine for each year that goes by—not from intellectual argument, but from personal experience. The very nature of what is happening apparently requires the shift to come from within, and not from external intellectualizing. Once the shift occurs, one is changed forever. It is likely that the tendency will accelerate and that we will eventually reach a critical mass that will make a global transformation possible, probably within the lifetime of the current generation.

For me, the most important result of my Indian experience was the return of my optimism about the future. The very fact that such a state of consciousness exists was personal proof for me that we will all experience it eventually. And what a different world that will be! In that state, emotions like hate, fear, and anger simply do not exist, and everything is experienced with a delicious intensity.

A second important result was the realization that really fundamental change in society can only come from below, from the people, the grass roots, and not from above. I had to admit that Hildur was right about this. Now, I would have to consider what this insight meant to my own future actions.

While there are many uncertainties, we seem to be approaching some kind of climax in our evolution. Some have called it a birth process, which feels right to me, and was close to my vision of the emerging butterfly. I think it will affect every person on the planet sooner or later, and very dramatically. Each will have to make an individual choice. Choose sides, so to speak: the spiritual or the material. But actually this is an over-simplification, because it is not so much a choice between the two as an integration of the two that is the true task. Ungrounded spirituality is as false a path as godless materialism.

Indeed, the main question I asked myself after my experience in India was precisely that: how do I integrate my newly found spiritual insight into my everyday life? This is the question that everyone should ask themselves. Everyone who makes the paradigm shift in the coming years will have to face the same question. Each answer will be different, depending on each person's situation, potential, and abilities. No one can say: I am too weak, or too poor, or too helpless. Mother Theresa's example should be enough to dispel that notion.

Muktananda's words "Start with yourself" are very important too. It can be a very tempting response to try to change the external world or other people's behavior. What is far more important and far more difficult is to look at one's own life and make changes there. In my own case, it was far from clear to me what the consequences would be when I returned from India. One immediate action was to move my office from downtown Copenhagen to my home. I was fortunate in that computer technology allowed me to do so. It didn't really matter where I was located anymore.

5

The Forex Jungle

After my return to Denmark from Muktananda, the "altered state" gradually wore off over a period of a few days. I found it was extremely difficult to maintain it in the face of normal, everyday family life with three children. While the experience affected me deeply, I did not understand what it meant, and needed time to investigate, read, and think it all through. In the meantime I had my business to think of.

In the mid-1970s Peter and I had sold off our consulting operations, or more to the point, had given them away, after ten years in the fast lane. The fact was that things were not going well. Business was in a downturn. Our investments in the future were taking much longer than expected to materialize. Peter and I had gone for two years without drawing a salary, and our capital was almost gone due to the under-capitalization caused by the Palby disaster. Besides which Peter had picked up some mysterious tropical disease in Bangla Desh that limited him to a two-hour work day. It was time to bail out while we could still maneuver. Peter wanted to return to his academic career, and I wanted to have a simple one-man operation where I could control all aspects of my consulting jobs, preferably operating out of my home where I could be close to the family. I also wanted to specialize in just one area, finance, rather than be spread out over a range of different industries.

Initially, my focus was on portfolio theory applied to managing large investment portfolios. My customers were mostly banks, insurance companies and pension funds in Scandinavia and the UK. In the early 1980s, the emphasis shifted to the foreign exchange market, which I began researching in depth in 1980-82. Thus one of the first tasks at hand upon my return from India was putting the final touches on my new currency forecasting system.

At first glance, nothing seems more remote from spirituality than the world of high finance. Yet the next few years saw me splitting my time between these two worlds. I often laughed inwardly at the thought of how the people of my two worlds would react if they saw me in the other half. Occasionally they would overlap and I would discuss the other world with an acquaintance. But for the most part, they were quite separate.

My heart was not in the currency market. To me it was just a numbers game with a certain intellectual challenge. But I had to make a living, and selling my forecasting system had certain advantages. One was that I could automate it, thereby minimizing the time I had to spend on routine operations. I set up the system on the internationally accessible I.P. Sharp computer network (later taken over by Reuters) in such a way that the raw data and all the model's parameters and forecasts were updated daily on the mainframe in Toronto without any human intervention. The forecasting system was quite general in that it could be used with any domestic currency as reference. As it was available by local telephone call in 500 cities world-wide, it was a quite unique electronic product. Once set up, it could in principle go on forever without intervention. This had its advantages when I was traveling or on holidays. Clients simply called in on a limited access number and got a printout as often as needed. In fact, I didn't even know what was being recommended to my clients unless I specifically wanted to know. The system was fully automatic. In the early days it could be accessed by a telex machine or intelligent terminal or personal computer— though the latter were not widespread until the mid eighties. All I had to do was send out a once-a-month performance report and invoices. Most of my time was thus spent promoting the system to potential clients.

Until I started traveling around selling my system, I hadn't spent much time with the people actually making currency decisions in the banks, investment companies, and major corporations. I had done my research pretty much in isolation. It was quite a learning experience, and shocking in one respect. In those days, very few of the people responsible for major decisions on currency exposure had a sufficient background, overview, and mentality to handle their jobs responsibly. It was a time for on-the-job learning, and a lot of mistakes were made. After all, floating rates were a rather recent phenomenon, dating back to 1971, and nobody had experience in this new field. It looked easy on the surface but was in fact very difficult to master successfully. It was not at all surprising to me to hear about the highly publicized currency losses and scandals that filled the newspapers.

One would think that this would have made my sales pitch a little easier, but that was not the case. The Brits, for example, were generally a tough sell. They had the cynical attitude that "nobody gets it right" because, apparently, most of the UK merchant bank advisers had been getting the currency market consistently wrong for years. Old boy Brits would not dream of looking elsewhere, say to "Europe" or the USA for better advice due to their arrogant "not invented here" attitude. The irony was that they did not even know they were far behind their competitors in the States—and even in Scandinavia—in introducing computer technology into the world of finance. Their illusions were crushed after the "big bang" introduction of competitive pricing on the London Stock Exchange in the 1980s. The Americans moved in and forced the London financial community to adopt a normal working day for the first time ever. Financial executives began coming in early and eating home-made lunch packs in a half hour break in front of their screens like the rest of the world, instead of coming in at ten and taking off two hours for a three course meal at the private club, followed by 9 holes at the golf club, weather permitting. Now they stayed until six o'clock if they wanted to keep their jobs. They had to fight to stay in business. The three-martini lunch became a thing of the past. Many British financial institutions did not survive. Many that did were taken over by foreigners.

It is a common misunderstanding that banks are the best forecasters of currency trends. Not so! Banks earn their money on the spread between buying and selling, not by forecasting trends correctly. A major tactic for the really big banks in London is to utilize the customer orders coming in the morning from the Far East. That tells them which way the market is going to move that day, and so they adjust their own positions accordingly first—"standing in front of the wave" was the way one London banker described it to me in an unguarded moment. They are interested in turnover. Volume. Execution. Customer information. That is where they make their money. Generally speaking, they are not very good at forecasting at all. At least not beyond the next few minutes. This may come as a surprise to the man-in-the-street, but not to anyone who has worked in a trading room. In fact most bank traders are not even allowed to take positions of any size overnight. They "square the books" each evening before they go home. The exceptions are a small number of the very largest international banks, the so-called "market makers" that will quote tight two-way prices in almost any amount in the major currencies and put the positions on their own book—i.e., they do not have to pass them on to somebody else.

The other 99% of the world's banks pass on most of their customer deals to the market makers, and take a good chunk of the spread for themselves at no risk. It is no wonder that every little bank in the world tries to get a piece of the action. Most corporations do not deal directly with the market makers. One reason is size. The market makers will not accept you if you are too small. Another is captivity by domestic banks that typically have a lot of other business to intimidate their corporate clients with, like the line of credit. Another is ignorance of how they are getting ripped off. I was in this latter category for about two years before I learned the facts of life.

This understanding that trading volume and not forecasting was the prime business of banks came home to me very clearly at a meeting I held in New York with Citibank in the late eighties. They had just decided to close down their currency advising activities for two good reasons. Firstly because they had learned that outside specialists were better at it! Secondly, they said, it is bad business to risk losing a big client because he is angry about your causing him currency trading losses, which, though relatively small in the total relationship, are annoying to the customer and psychologically damaging to the bank's reputation. So their attitude was that they would rather refer customers that wanted currency advice to outside specialists as long as Citibank got the trading business. Very clever!

A concept that causes a lot of misunderstandings is the word "speculation." An old saw says that a speculation is an investment that went wrong. There is an element of truth in this. I know of no one that ever got fired for making a speculative profit (usually called an "astute investment" with hindsight). But the unemployment lists include thousands of people who made a "speculative" loss for their companies, again with hindsight. In reality, there is no substantive difference—at most perhaps a difference in the uncertainty of the outcome. The real difference is in the eyes of the beholder.

There is apparently a psychological need for many business leaders to call their speculations by some other name, or perhaps to redefine the concept entirely to fit their needs. Take, for example, the following incident. I had a meeting once with the highly respected Chief Executive of one of Denmark's largest companies, one with very substantial dollar-based raw material imports. He was representative of an attitude I have met on many occasions. I tried to interest him in using my methods to follow a selective cover policy on his dollar exposure, the choice of cover or not depending on my forecast model. (To "cover" means to enter a currency transaction that removes your exposure completely. It costs almost nothing, about 0.05% of the exposure.) "No," he replied firmly. "We understand our product, but we don't understand the currency market." He looked at me with a slightly disapproving frown. "We are not speculators," he claimed righteously. "Therefore we never cover."

I am not sure if I was more flabbergasted or amused. "But," I replied, "Do you not realize that by doing nothing you are a pure speculator? A more selective strategy could only reduce the amount of speculation you are already doing. You could cut your risk and save money as well."

"That's not the way I look at it," he said gravely, shifting uncomfortably in his chair. He obviously wasn't used to being called a speculator. "If I started covering risk in the currency market, and got it wrong—and let's face it, you cannot avoid getting it wrong some of the time—then I would be opening up myself for criticism from the board. It could cost me my job. As it is, the board has made a policy decision once and for all, on my recommendation, that this company does no hedging." Hedging is another word for covering your exposure.

If you are confused, it is not your fault. When he talks about "getting it wrong," he means missing a speculative profit that with hindsight he might have made. Many executives have indeed been fired by their boards for *not* speculating, i.e., for "getting it wrong"—believe it or not. Many!

That particular CEO's speculative policy cost his company more than $15 million as the dollar appreciated in 1980-83, and would cost another $15 million in the next two years as the dollar continued its upward flight. And he justified it by claiming he wasn't a speculator! What a topsy-turvy world! But his job was safe—that was the most important thing!

It is a curious, but common error in thinking to confuse selective cover (sometimes you cover, sometime you don't), which is a prudent strategy, with pure speculation, which means doing nothing about your natural exposure. It is also speculation to take on an exposure that you do not have to. Journalists often add to the confusion by buying into the myth that somewhere out there (the gnomes of Zurich? George Soros?) exist mysterious and evil "speculators" who are upsetting the normal course of business by manipulating the currency and undermining the Central Banks, responsible politicians, and hard-working businessmen.

Don't believe it! The fact is that the biggest speculators of all are the thousands of "hard working businessmen" who panic when they suspect that something is about to happen in the currency market and catch them with their pants down. They change their normal payment patterns in the so-called "leads and lags" phenomenon, and bring about the very crisis they fear. They act for the most part defensively, trying to protect themselves, and all at once, like lemmings, putting tremendous pressure on the currency. The really big professional speculators, in absolute terms, are the handful of gigantic market makers, often including the domestic banks of the very country whose currency is under pressure. They dwarf George Soros—even though he is quite large—as he himself has pointed out publicly.

For the information of the few who haven't heard, George Soros is known as "the man who broke the Bank of England" in the Sterling crisis of September, 1992, when he reputedly earned $1,000,000,000 dollars for his hedge fund by selling Sterling prior to its devaluation. This incident is often used by journalists to further the myth of the big, bad, speculator. In fact, Soros was just a messenger bringing the bad news—he was not the cause of the devaluation. The real cause was the unwillingness of the UK government to increase interest rates for domestic policy reasons. They wanted to have their cake and eat it too. Keep interest rates low to fuel economic growth, and keep the pound strong to avoid inflation. However, the latter task—keeping Sterling strong—they thought they could export to the German Bundesbank, which was obligated to intervene on Sterling's behalf according to the terms of the European Monetary System (EMS). But the Bundesbank was furious and would not play the Brits game unless they contributed something, in particular a healthy hike in UK interest rates. The UK refused, and the die was cast. The Bundesbank pulled out of the market and let Sterling collapse. Soros was astute in reading the situation correctly, but was not a prime cause. Nor was he alone. The major UK banks earned far more than Soros by selling their own currency. When the Bank of England finally did react with a 2% hike—it was too late to stem the flow. It is always this way.

Currency crises are *always* caused by politicians trying to peg their currency at an unrealistic exchange rates until it is forced to move suddenly in a crisis, instead of letting it gradually shift in a free floating environment. Speculators at most help to tip a falling wagon, and in normal markets are actually supporting the weakest currencies of the deficit countries trying to pick up the interest differential. Indeed that is their economic raison d'être—to clear the market so supply equals demand. The currency market is greatly misunderstood by the public, as well as by most economists. I was also confused at first, and it took me years of intensive study and trading experience to figure out what was really going on.

I spent about two years traveling around Europe selling my forecasting system, picking up a respectable number of clients, but also meeting substantial resistance from many businessmen, including many traders who did not have an adequate understanding of the market or the risks they were taking. It was the Wild West in modern choreography those days, with yuppie golden boys in their Porsches taking on the role of the gunslingers. Most of them were utter disasters for their companies. This was the market I call the forex jungle (forex = foreign exchange in the market slang). The market and most of the people trading in it were undisciplined, unprofessional, unsophisticated, over-confident, and inexperienced—a disastrous combination. It lasted throughout the eighties and early nineties, and changed only gradually. A shake-out occurred as the currency loss disasters followed each other on the front pages like a repeating nightmare: Freddie Laker, British Aerospace, Jaguar, Volkswagen, Lufthansa, Boliden, Sony, and on and on in a never-ending story. For every one that made the papers, there were ten that were kept discreetly silent.

By the end of 1983, I was tiring of the repetitive nature of my business, especially the many rejections. Every month I would send out about fifty thick envelopes to clients and prospects with detailed analyses, performance reports, etc. One day, my son Fry was asked at his kindergarten what his father did for a living. "He sells paper," said Fry.

That was bad enough. But then, a few weeks later, while in London, after a long, hard day of presentations and no successes, my final meeting was with a very arrogant British banker, who, it turned out, was only interested in picking my brain, and not in doing business. As I was leaving, his parting shot to me was: "Dr. Jackson, if your system is so bloody good, why are you selling it?." I returned, rather annoyed, to my hotel. But his comment kept echoing in my head until I realized that he was absolutely right. I should be using my system to trade my own money. If my figures were right, it would be a much more profitable business, even with the limited capital I had saved up. I was through using my valuable time trying to convince skeptical businessmen that they could earn a lot of money using my system. The thought of being free of all that aggravation was a driving factor.

Another factor that influenced my decision was a change of law as of January, 1984, that allowed Danish companies for the first time to deal in currency options. This was part of the gradual liberalization of capital flows that took place in Europe during the 1980s, and was a recognition of this new financial vehicle that had quite recently become very popular internationally. It just happened that options—though quite new to most people in the market, were an old specialty of mine, going back to my Ph.D. thesis almost twenty years earlier. I had been one of the very first to do serious research in the area that came to be known as financial derivatives. That was almost ten years before the

Chicago Options Board Exchange began to list equity options, and almost twenty years before currency options hit the mainstream. So it would be fun, I thought, to dust off the old equations and adapt them to the currency market.

Besides, the idea of buying options appealed to me because of the limited risk and the simplicity of management—an important factor in my one-man operation. When you buy an option, you can at most lose your premium, which is the fixed cost of entering the transaction. The idea of an option is that you purchase the right, but not the obligation, to use it—i.e., to buy and sell simultaneously a particular currency pair at a particular price, say the US Dollar versus the Yen at 110 Yen per Dollar, within the agreed time frame, typically one month. Trading options successfully is not a trivial matter, requiring extensive computer software, a mathematical theory, sophisticated estimation techniques for currency "volatilities" (a fluctuation measure) and trends, and a strategy for trading and risk control.

Interestingly, Myron Scholes and Robert Merton won the Nobel prize in economics in 1997 for their derivation of the widely used "Black-Scholes" option pricing model in 1970, illustrating how important this field has become in the 1990s. The third man who would have participated, Fisher Black, died in 1995. Curiously, their option pricing model differed very little from the formula used in my Ph.D. thesis in 1964, and by others before me. But their derivation of the formula was certainly very elegant.

I will not bore the non-technical reader with more details about options. It is not critical to my story. Suffice it to say that currency options were right down my alley. I had all the necessary historical data in the computer already. And so I had an operational model in place within about four months, and I began testing the validity of my model in the real marketplace in May, 1984, using my company's $100,000 liquid capital as a stake.

6

Rainbow Bank

In October, 1984 I attended an international conference on "One Earth" at Findhorn in northern Scotland as part of my ongoing search for a better understanding of my Indian experience. Findhorn is a small spiritual community founded in 1962, that calls itself the first "planetary village." It was at the time, and remains today, a place to come for inspiration for those whose interests include spirituality, evolving consciousness, personal development, the paradigm shift and related topics. A feature is the beautiful Universal Hall, ideally suited for such conferences.

It was indeed an inspiring occasion for me, as I met a number of people who thought along similar lines, and who also had had unusual spiritual experiences. One very inspiring person was Josè Lutzenburger from Brazil, who stayed in the same bungalow. He was a one-man army, who had taken on the Brazilian power structure that was destroying the environment, putting his life literally on the line. He would later become the Minister of Environment in an ironic turn of events. He gave a passionate presentation called "Gaian Economics," emphasizing the need to integrate ecology into our economic planning, reinforcing my own thinking.

One of the workshops that also made an impression on me concerned alternative banking. There was a tremendous need for financing of projects that did not meet the traditional banks' criteria. Alternative banks like Mercury Provident in the UK and Triodos in Belgium were showing that it could be done.

But the thing that struck me most while there was that there were so many people who were both spiritually motivated and activists in their daily lives, putting the two dimensions together in a balanced fashion. They were from all walks of life and worked in many different ways. There were also many that were unbalanced, but they only emphasized the need to stay grounded. So I came away convinced that the proper way to use one's spiritual inspiration was to integrate it into one's everyday life, whatever one's talents or position might be, and use it actively to make this a better world. Thus I returned to Denmark with the feeling that I had done enough thinking, talking, and reading. It was time to take some action.

Soon after my return, an opportunity arose at a public meeting called by an NGO Hildur was working with called The Nordic Alternative Campaign. The objective of this project was to raise $14 million from the Nordic parliaments to carry out research jointly by grass roots organizations—100 of them were associated with the project—and traditional university researchers, in order to develop and describe a global vision integrating social, ecological and economic solutions in an alternative vision based on cooperation between North and South economies, as opposed to the traditional economic growth model.

I put forward the idea of a grass roots project to raise $3.5 million (the legal minimum) to form an alternative Danish bank which I suggested we call Gaia Bank. The project would have a double objective: (1) to raise consciousness about our relationship to money (2) to create, if successful, a source of capital independent of the traditional channels that could finance worthwhile projects that would not normally receive traditional bank loans.

The response was quite positive, and a subsequent meeting was called with a number of key people whom the network thought might be interested in the idea, including two existing alternative banks. I had nothing against either of the existing banks, who were both very sympathetic to our goals, but felt that what was needed was a fresh impulse from a broadly based grass roots movement that was national, more ambitious and non-sectarian. It was agreed to form a committee and call a founding meeting in early Spring 1985.

The founding meeting was well attended, with over 100 people from all over Denmark, and was given reasonable press coverage. We were off to a good start, with a secretariat in Aarhus and several active regional groups. The business plan was to have interested shareholders make a commitment for one or more shares at $150 per share paid up front. The money would be deposited with a savings bank for safe custody, and the association would receive the interest on the deposit in order to finance the campaign. In the event that the minimum capital was not committed by the end of 1986, all money would be returned but without accrued interest. The savings bank agreed to lend the association funds based on the indicated interest stream and personal guarantees from the board, which included myself as treasurer. Our basic operating idea for the bank was to have very few branches, just one in each of four or five regional centers. With the use of modern computers, the telephone, and the post offices for deposits and, it was no longer necessary in our opinion to have an extensive and costly retail branch network. The lower costs could make the project profitable and competitive.

Interestingly, we hit the nail on the head with that insight, which was quite novel at the time. In subsequent years, all the major banks did indeed shut down a substantial part of their branch networks to save costs. It became more and more common to do all your banking electronically without ever entering the branch where your account was. Indeed, these days, some Internet banks have no branches! On the whole it was a good and viable plan, considering we had no capital to work with. But we were very dependent on free press coverage and a successful start in the first six months so that we could finance the campaign.

The key to success was how many people would respond to our appeal. There was no doubt that the people who generally sympathized with our objectives had the financial clout to make it work if they could coordinate their efforts, even though they are a very small part of the population. Our target group were people who were opposed to many things that were being financed by their own money at their traditional banks—things such as toxic chemicals polluting the ground water, pesticides, weapons, tobacco, chemical fertilizers, property speculation, and much more. What more logical thing to do than pull out your money and put it somewhere else that has a more socially responsible loan policy? But how many people make the connection between their modest bank account and all the things happening around them that they would like to see changed? Most people are not aware how important they are for the banking system. There was only one way to find out if the concept would fly, and that was to try it and see.

This was my first experience working with a grass roots project, and it was a mixed pleasure. On the one hand, it was inspiring to work with so many volunteer workers, who were ideologically motivated. On the other hand, it was often frustrating and time-consuming getting decisions made by the traditional grass roots consensus method. One thing I was a little disappointed with was the treatment of my name proposal—Gaia Bank. It turned out that the name Gaia had not yet penetrated the Danish scene the way it had internationally. So it was democratically voted down in favor of "Rainbow Bank," a name I thought was slightly frivolous, as well as being risky from a marketing point of view. As it turned out, the name did turn off a lot of people, who might have gone into a project they considered serious.

I was also to experience another phenomenon typical for grass roots projects—fractions based on different ideologies. One subgroup was primarily interested in the idea of eliminating interest rates, and saw the project as a vehicle to promote their cause. They fought long and hard to put their views across in strategy meetings, in brochure drafts, and in interviews with the press. I had no ideological view on the issue, but pragmatically could see that it was too narrow a concept to attract a broad range of investors, and it would merely confuse our message. Besides which there was no way I could get the numbers to work without interest income. Much time was wasted debating. I slowly came to realize that a lot of the participants were more interested in the discussions than in making the project a success.

In the event, we failed to generate enough momentum in the first six months to fuel the locomotive, in spite of good press coverage and in spite of having salaried staff and volunteers in several regional centers. There were many enthusiastic supporters, but not enough to generate anything like $3.5 million.

We discovered that there is a long way between talking and opening your wallet for most people. For example, a couple who were quite close friends of ours were typical in their reaction. For years they had loudly supported all the popular causes on the political left, voted Socialist, etc., while frowning at my capitalist leanings. They thought Rainbow Bank was a "great initiative," but they had a liquidity problem. They could not find the necessary $150, what with two cars, a big mortgage on their villa, a summer cottage to keep up, and their obligatory ski vacation in southern Europe. Sorry. "But it is a great idea, Ross."

Perhaps we were too early out. Perhaps we were naïve to expect people to see the connection between their bank accounts and the developments in society which they opposed. We certainly underestimated the difficulty of getting people to consider switching banks, that for many people represent an almost religious authority. For sure we were undercapitalized. But at least, in the end, we had the satisfaction of knowing that we had made the attempt, and had conceded defeat honorably. Everyone got their deposits back. No one suffered any losses. And we were all one experience richer and a little wiser.

For me, the message was that if I was going to do something meaningful, it would have to be based on whatever resources I could muster on my own. I had had enough of the grass roots approach, and enough of fund raising. An alternative possibility that I had not foreseen even one year earlier was emerging in my mind even as the Rainbow Bank project was winding up, and it depended on no one but myself to make it work.

7

The Money Machine

I never considered myself a currency trader. My strength was analysis and software development. Since my disaster with Palsby back in 1968, I had never invested in the stock market, or any other market. Any savings I had, and they were not much, had gone into conservative bonds.

I adopted what I considered to be a conservative strategy, committing only ten percent of my capital at a time for a one month period to buy the best options according to my computer analysis. I could at most lose ten percent of my capital in a given month. My analysis indicated that I could expect to earn about 6% per month on my capital, assuming my estimates of volatility and trend would continue to be as much better than the market's as they had been in the test period. I was very excited about finding out if the real world behaved as my theory said it would.

With $100,000 to work with and a typical one month option costing about 1% of the underlying exposure, I could spend roughly $10,000 per month on premium (i.e., option purchases), corresponding to about one million dollars of exposure. With a shaking hand I put on my first option in May 1984 for about $2500. Thereafter I systematically put on one option a week and put them away in the drawer to await expiration day, without worrying about what was happening in the meantime. For me, trading options was like playing craps with loaded dice, where I had a slight edge, but would still lose my entire "bet" about 45% of the time. That uncertainty can be very unnerving to some people. But personally, I decided from the very start that I would regard it unemotionally as a game of bets that might work and might not, so it never bothered me. I had no personal prestige tied up in it, and could walk away from it with no regrets if it didn't seem to work. Aside from my banking contacts, very few people had any idea what I was doing.

It was some years later that I learned that nobody else traded options the way I did. Most professionals at the banks are actually sellers of options. When they do buy, they tend to monitor their positions on a continual basis on their Reuters screens, trading against them in the currency market to cut losses or lock in profits. That was not my style. I was too busy with other things in my one-man operation and had neither the time nor the inclination to follow the minute by minute fluctuations on a Reuters screen. Indeed I never had a Reuters screen, then or later. I used at most a half day a week putting on my trades and keeping track of them on my computer.

As the months progressed I had some unexpected experiences. One thing that surprised me was the tremendous differences in the prices quoted at different banks for the same option. I was able to exploit that in a way that would not be possible years later when the market became much more efficient. But in 1984, it was still the forex jungle. Many currency traders had no idea of the risks they were taking.

By late 1986, I had enough evidence to see that my trading strategy was making a return on capital in line with my theoretical expectations—over 100% per annum. I had built up a capital of about $400,000 and began to think about next steps. It was about this time that the Rainbow Bank project was winding up, and I began wondering if there wasn't another away of accomplishing some of the same objectives using currency trading. I could of course, simply keep trading my own money. But there was a much quicker way to accumulate money. Trade *other* people's money as well, for a share of their profits, earning a so-called incentive fee. I did some simulations of the expected profits that might be generated. The numbers were staggering. If you can double your capital every year, you can become very big very fast. I said to myself: these numbers are so powerful that I have to give it a try.

I approached a number of Danish banks with the idea of a joint venture investment company based on this concept. They would raise the money and it would be traded according to my system. But the reaction was uniformly the same. An excellent idea, but why should we do it with you when we have the same expertise in house? The fact that none of them *had* the same expertise, knowledge, research capability or documented track record did not deter them. They were, after all, sitting on the distribution network, and hence the customers, which in their view was much more important than the content of the product. Unfortunately for the average investor, they had a valid point.

After many rejections, even by middle-sized provincial banks that were way over their heads, it became clear to me that if the concept were to work it would have to be done outside of Denmark in the so-called offshore market, and without the benefit of the distribution channels of the banks, who would simply view me as competition. We would have to do our own distribution. Thus was born the basic idea of Gaiacorp as a vertically integrated currency manager marketing an investment vehicle based exclusively on OTC ("over-the-counter," i.e., through banks as opposed to exchange-listed future contracts) currency trading. No such company existed anywhere at the time.

An essential part of my thinking was the ownership structure. I wanted the benefits, if any, to accrue primarily to the environmental movement, to the movement towards sustainability. My idea was to have a charitable foundation own Gaiacorp, as my way of integrating spirituality and materialism. It would be ironic indeed if I were able to extract money from the currency market and divert it to useful purposes benefiting the planet. There were so many good people and projects out there that lacked capital. If my numbers were right, there was an opportunity here to make a difference. I had to find out!

Hildur and I discussed the idea in late 1986. She was very skeptical, and did what she could to discourage me, primarily because of her experience with a small, private foundation, where she had been a board member for three years, distributing funds to small, alternative projects. She and the other board members had all become very frustrated with the process. They had very few funds to distribute, and seemed to be creating a lot of disappointment and bitterness among those who did not receive grants, while those who did always got less than they wanted and were not satisfied either. It was also very time-consuming for the board. Finally, the board decided to give all the remaining funds to one project to try to make a difference, and then closed down the foundation. The chosen project turned out to be a fiasco.

I argued that my vision was to do things differently. The foundation would be proactive, focusing its funds in a few well chosen initiatives that it had a degree of control over, rather than distributing them in the traditional way. In early 1987 Hildur and I called together a dozen or so friends whom we felt shared our vision. Together about ten of us founded Gaia Trust as a cooperative entity with charitable objectives, with each person contributing the symbolic amount of $150 for a share. No member, including myself, could ever benefit personally, either through capital gain or dividends, but rather, each would act like a trustee, electing the board, approving overall strategy, and assuring that the Articles of Association were upheld. I felt that this was a more stable and more democratic structure for a holding company than a foundation, which always runs the risk of being side-tracked and taken over by a self-appointed board.

I pointed out to the others that I considered this a forty year project. We had to think in terms of long term stable structures. Perhaps none of us would still be around at the end of that period. I proposed that Gaia Trust hold 90% of the shares of Gaiacorp, and I would keep 10% for myself.

I set up a small working group in London in the summer of 1987 to launch the Gaiacorp project. The basic idea was to sell shares in a mutual fund based on currency trading, using my track record. We would sell it primarily as a diversification element in institutional or large private investment portfolios. We could show that a currency portfolio was uncorrelated with returns on stocks and bonds, an important argument for investing a small percentage in this new asset class. I chose as members of that initial group some people I knew through the green network, rather than experienced professionals. This turned out to be a rather naïve idea on my part, but at the time I hoped to build Gaiacorp with people who were of high integrity, spiritually motivated, and good businessmen. I was later to learn that this was a rare combination indeed, so rare as to be almost non-existent.

We agreed from the start that we would not mention the connection with Gaia Trust unless specifically asked. We did not want to create an image of Gaiacorp as a warm and fuzzy environmentalist firm appealing to people's consciences, but rather as a top professional firm that was a leader in its field.

The group's major task was to raise a minimum of $5 million as required by UK law for the two investment funds, which we decided would be called Gaia Hedge I and Gaia Hedge II, with different risk profiles. If we didn't raise the minimum, the money raised would have to be given back. Other tasks included a lot of legal work, which is very expensive in London, preparation of marketing materials, an advertising campaign, and setting up administrative systems. None of the others had any capital, so all the costs had to be covered by my firm, but would be recoverable from the two public funds if we got our minimum. I didn't see this as a big risk initially because I figured I could raise double that much on my own just from my own contacts in London and Copenhagen, particularly from two large UK institutions whom I had informally sounded out already and got what I considered a gentleman's agreement of backing.

But trouble was brewing. Murphy's law was at work. Everything was taking more time than planned. Legal problems continued to pop up. The lawyers didn't understand currencies and options, which were new to them. My "green" team was unable to deliver the goods. We were doing so many things that had never been done before that many mistakes were made, time was lost, and expenses piled up. The critical deadline to receive the minimum was the end of April 1988. It couldn't be postponed because my money was running out, all $400,000 of it. The prospectus and brochures came out too late. Very few of the "green" group's investment contacts materialized. We had a communication problem with potential investors as we were breaking new ground. Nobody had previously looked at currencies as an investment. Nobody understood options. We invited many UK institutions to sophisticated presentations, but few bit. They either didn't understand or wanted to see a three year track record before committing. I began to get concerned.

Then, as the deadline approached, one of my "certain" UK backers, a major insurance group, decided not to invest as expected. My other major backer was still on, but another problem arose. An obscure paragraph in UK law that none of our lawyers told us about would prevent the funds having more than 50% UK investors. Indeed I found the clause myself after spending just two hours reading a UK law book. I was furious at the poor legal advice we were getting. The UK was where we had put all our marketing effort, and now, suddenly the non-U.K. institutions were critical to our success. We would need at least $2.5 million from my Danish contacts and time was short. After an intensive effort I managed to line up the necessary commitments from Danish clients who had seen my system in practice and had confidence in me. It looked like we would just make it.

As we approached the final deadline when money had to actually be transferred to the custodian bank, I called each of the major investors just to make sure that everything was happening according to plan. Normally that should not be necessary with institutional investors. But as it turned out, my intuition was right. One institution had forgotten the date of the commitment. Another couldn't get its fax to work internationally (they were quite new those days) and was ready to give up until I had them fax to me instead and I passed the instructions on. Incredible! Another couldn't understand the English instructions and was also prepared to drop the task without calling me. I was shocked. But in the end it all worked out. But only because nothing was taken for granted. The whole project was within an eyelash of failing, and my company with it.

By May, 1988 Gaiacorp was a reality. I had done my last trade in the currency market. From now on it was up to Gaiacorp's professional traders to carry on from where I had left off. Within three years Gaiacorp became a very successful and well-known player in the international currency market, worth over $20 million, and became one of the largest currency option buyers in the market. Later it had a rocky period for a while as the nature of the market shifted and the EMS broke up. But it recovered, and the charitable program was never greatly affected.

Ironically, by the early 1990s, Gaia Trust had more than enough funds to start Rainbow Bank all by itself. However, by that time, one of the Danish alternative banks, had grown from its regional base in Northern Jutland, and had widened its original anthroposophic (Rudolf Steiner) vision to something very close to our ideal in the Rainbow Bank project. So I decided instead to back this little bank with a substantial capital infusion—on condition that they change their name to the more user-friendly "Mercury Bank" and step up their marketing efforts. Since then, Mercury Bank has been growing very rapidly, has become the bank of choice of the alternative movement in Denmark, and is doing very well financially, also.

So, in one sense, the Rainbow Bank project did after all have a happy ending.

8

Gaia Trust

Developing a strategy to use the funds becoming available was to a great extent a question of Hildur and I reaching agreement on a platform, although other members participated in the discussions as well. We were coming from very different starting points, she as a grass roots activist with a background in the women's movement, the peace movement, and the Nordic Alternative Campaign (an attempt to tackle the "social, ecological and global problems" facing Mankind). I was coming from a management consultant background with a specialty in operations research, combined with the spiritual insights of my Indian experience. In common we had 20 years of positive experience in one of the first cohousing projects, and some negative, but valuable, experiences with the Rainbow Bank project.

In spite of her quasi-Marxist background and my many years of working in the capitalist world of TNCs (transnational corporations) and major financial institutions, we agreed essentially on an analysis of what was happening in the world and why.

Twentieth century society had evolved into a system which seemed to be out of control and leading to disaster in one form or another in a matter of decades at most. Looking at the planet as a whole, one could see almost a third in desperate conditions, not knowing where the next meal was coming from, an increasing number migrating to the slums of the exploding mega-cities of the South with no water supply and rampant disease everywhere. At the opposite extreme, the affluent societies of North America, Western Europe, and Japan, in spite of their economic success, were in many ways even worse off.

Families were disintegrating; violence, sickness and drugs were on the increase. The middle classes were disappearing as the cleft between rich and poor continued to widen both within countries and between countries. The environment was being degraded faster and faster in the

name of economic growth. Species were disappearing at a phenomenal rate as if there were no tomorrow. The air, water, and soil were
being poisoned by the by-products of "progress." The future was shap-
ing up as a violent competition for a rapidly diminishing supply of
essential resources.

A visitor from another planet would observe that there was no
political leadership in this world. It was every nation for itself. The
United Nations had no global mandate, but was rather a debating club
for nations, conveniently ignored when vital national interests were
threatened. Many politicians at the nation state level were primarily
interested in lining there own pockets and protecting the interests of
the corporate clients who financed their election. Not only in the South,
which had a long tradition of corruption, but increasingly in Europe
and North America. Democracy was becoming a sham. The real power
now resided with the TNCs that were the only truly global players.
Scandals and exposés of political and business corruption were everyday news. The people have lost confidence in their political leaders. It
was beginning to look like democracy in its original sense was in danger of dying, with only the formality of the casting of ballots remaining. In short the politicians had no intention whatsoever of bringing
about real reforms that would move us towards a sustainable, equitable
world. However, there was no shortage of platitudes and lofty declarations.

Under these conditions, on which we generally concurred, it was
only a question of time before a breakdown occurred. The current
growth path was obviously unsustainable. Change was most unlikely to
come from the top down, for the reasons mentioned above. Either
there would be a fundamental breakdown, in all likelihood triggered
by a financial collapse, or there would evolve an alternative culture
from below. In either case Mankind's future would have to be based
on living sustainably on the planet, nourishing the remaining resources
in a circulatory system without waste.

The question of why this situation has evolved has many aspects.
At the most fundamental level, the spiritual level, it is related to our losing contact with the divine. We have forgotten our divine origins and
lost ourselves in a hopeless struggle to satisfy our needs with material
things that can never fulfill that purpose. Eventually we will learn this
lesson, but we have much pain to go through first.

At a macro-economic level, what we are experiencing is reaching
the physical limits of the possibilities of a finite planet. Unfortunately,
our political, economic, and social experiences have not prepared us
for this new situation. Our elected leaders continue to promote the

solutions which were appropriate in a smaller world with regional powers, new frontiers and apparently unlimited resources—hence the religion of economic growth as the dominating political idea of our age. It is extremely difficult to abandon a strategy that has been so successful. And, like so many corporations that have been through the same evolution, the most likely scenario for the planet is that we will continue on the same path until a collapse occurs. We tend to learn the hard way. However, it does not necessarily have to go that way. If enough people choose a different path, a sustainable planet might evolve without collapse.

It was with this background of common thinking that we developed what we called our "yin yang" strategy for Gaia Trust, that is to say, equal parts of the feminine and masculine. We agreed that current society had far too much of the masculine, as seen in the emphasis on economic growth, hard science, and centralized planning. The feminine side was suffering. Social structure was being ignored. The traditional family structure was fragmenting. People were being atomized as consumers of products of industry. More and more functions were being taken over by the public sector, disempowering the individual. Rural societies, which had functioned well for centuries, were being destroyed in the name of economic efficiency, forcing migration to the cities, many of which, in the South, were on the verge of collapse. In the North, they were at best impersonal and unsafe.

We seemed to have forgotten that humans are social animals. For millennia we have lived in tribes and small communities. In our eagerness to improve physical living conditions, we ignored the human need for "community." So we built multi-storied apartment buildings where the facilities were better, but your next-door neighbor was a stranger. We built sleepy suburbs without social structure where nothing happens.

As concerned Gaia Trust policies, I convinced the others to accept a major principle that I felt strongly about. Gaia Trust should be proactive, that is to say, defining its own projects rather than just passively distributing grants. I felt there was a real need for an entity that could take on more sizable projects that no one else would or could fund. In other words, we should not do things that others are already doing, but look for areas where a focused effort could make a difference, even with the limited resources at our disposal.

Some of the others felt that it would be wrong to cut out grants entirely, as small amounts can often make a very big difference to people struggling with good ideas and no support. Also, grants would show the outside world something of what Gaia Trust stood for, and could be started right away. So we decided that we would allocate 10% of the yearly liquidity budget to grants. We continued this policy until we went onto the Internet in 1995 and had to cease because we could no longer handle the volume of applications.

So how do you go about creating a proactive strategy for change under these circumstances? We were talking about major change, long term fundamental change—nothing less than a new culture with new values. How do you bring it about? Is it even possible, with so many forces opposed? Are we just dreaming?

One of the first ideas put forward by some of the members was to form a "think tank" that would recruit some of the best people available and put them onto the task. We would seek support from or joint-venture with existing foundations in the UK and America. The idea would be to influence governmental thinking and public opinion.

However, neither Hildur nor I was convinced of this approach. It assumes governments are capable of bringing about radical change from the top down, and we both felt that was a naïve idea, and counter to our historical observations. New movements almost always originated with small groups operating from below the visible power structures.

Someone asked me to put on my professional operations research hat, and ask myself how I would tackle such a problem if I were asked by a client. An interesting question, and I thought hard about it. The OR approach is to define a problem precisely without any prejudice about how to solve it. If you are not careful, you can waste a lot of time and money on *apparent* problems that turn out to be something quite different. In OR theory, there have to be four elements present to have a "problem" in a given environment: a state of uncertainty about what to do, at least two alternatives, a decision-maker with the power to implement, and a criterion by which to distinguish alternative solutions. It is quite amazing how much time and energy can be wasted trying to come to grips with situations where one of the above ingredients is ill-defined or missing. You can have lots of aggravation, frustration, and dissatisfaction without having a "problem." For example, you may have no real alternatives!

I came quickly to the conclusion that the analysis and solution aspect was the least problematic part of the challenge. The most critical issue for me was: who is my client? Without knowing that, the question is academic. Without a decision-maker having the power to implement, we have no problem at all, only a "question" with many answers. A question can be interesting, and you can have a lot of fun and spend a lot of money analyzing answers. But you are not solving anybody's "problem." There was only one conceivable decision-maker that had the power to implement a top down global solution, I said.

"The United Nations?" asked someone. No, no, I said, they don't have any power at all. It would have to be some kind of TNC governance body with the mandate to take action on its members' behalf—something which does not exist today, and if it did, would be strongly opposed to the kind of changes that are needed. That's the bad news.

But the good news is that we know what the problems are and we know the solutions. We have all the necessary knowledge. We have the technology. It is a question of *implementation,* that faces us, not further analysis.

Thus did Hildur and I reach agreement on what Gaia Trust should do. She, using her feminine grass roots intuition, I, first after an intellectual exercise in fundamental problem-solving theory. It was obvious! We should *support the people who are intentionally living sustainably already.* Namely, the people who are building ecovillages around the world. Make them more visible. Promote the good examples. Make them into a movement, a global network whose members learn and gain strength from each other. Let them show others how it is done, so that when the time comes, they will know where to go, what to do.

The logic is simple. If the examples are good enough, they will be replicated. From then on, it is only a question of time until the strategy succeeds and ecovillages become the basis for a new culture based on a new holistic paradigm. The only uncertainty is the time it will take. Ecovillages are ideal vehicles for this task because they are by definition holistic, representing all the different aspect of sustainability in one place where it can be seen in an integrated solution—renewable energy, organic food production, a social network, waste water treatment, ecological building, and so on. It may take 20 years to become main stream, it may take much more, but it is inevitable. And if the examples are not good enough? Then we will simply have to help make them better!

Hildur was especially emphatic about the social dimension being the most important characteristic of an ecovillage—the reestablishment of community. As time has passed, I agree more and more with that early observation, although initially I was more focused on environmental sustainability. However, social networks are critical to the concept. Without this component, you do not have the necessary "glue" to create a common vision. Our cohousing experience taught us that. Without the "glue" you get a bunch of buildings with no soul. We tend to underestimate the importance of informal social networks in the West. They have disappeared to a great extent, especially in the big cities. But they are still of fundamental importance in the "developing countries." (Hildur hates that expression. "They are every bit as developed as we are." But what do you call them. The South? The Third World? There is no good answer.) We were recently in St. Petersburg, where many people had not received their salaries for 9 months, and there is nothing remotely resembling the Scandinavian welfare state. But the people survive because of their networks, sharing the little they have among family and friends. It is the same throughout the South.

One of the issues we discussed was the very term "ecovillage." It is a quite new expression that is just beginning to enter the mainstream vocabulary. This has the advantage that we can adopt it and define what it means. Make it *our* word. Its first usage as far as we could tell was in some of the recent issues of *In Context* magazine, the leading-edge periodical focusing on sustainability issues, used to describe some newer projects that went beyond cohousing to include food production in rural settings. The alternative mainstream name "sustainable communities" was already so misused that it often included traditional "economically" sustainable communities, Chamber of Commerce job creation projects and much more in a grab bag of usage, including much larger development projects than we envisioned. The best arguments in favor of "ecovillage" as a name was that it was catchy, undefined, and had positive overtones.

But we would have to define it to include inner city settlements in spite of its slightly rural image. Otherwise people would say we are ignoring half the population. Were there any examples of good inner city projects, we wondered? And where are the best examples of ecovillages anyway? The best source of information at the time was "Builders of the Dawn," but it was already several years old, and heavily American in content.[1]

We called Robert and Diane Gilman in Seattle to find out. They were the founder/editors of *In Context* magazine, and had visited us recently in Copenhagen. But they had no quick and easy answers. Which led us to our first major decision to use funds in Gaia Trust. We commissioned Robert and Diane to do a worldwide survey in order to describe the status quo of the ecovillage phenomenon, and in particular, to identify the best examples. We decided to establish a new entity called Gaia Villages to carry out the strategy. It would be a division of Gaia Trust with separate books and budgets.

That was the feminine "yin" part of the strategy. The other string on the bow was the masculine "yang" part—job creation. A fundamental problem with the ecovillage concept was financial. How would people make their livings in an ecovillage so they could afford to make the move? Ideally, most should work close to home or in the home. This is a vital part of the concept of reduced transportation and re-establishing local community. Otherwise you end up with a sleepy commuters' village or worse. Modern trends were actually moving in our favor, with the new possibilities opened up by the personal computer. I had myself been one of the first, in 1982, to move my computer-based business into my home outside the city. There was also a trend to a greater number of self-employed people with one-man/woman businesses, and more part-time jobs were being created. All these trends were in our favor. How could we best help things along so more people could have the option of moving into an ecovillage? What about production jobs?

A key element in a sustainable community is to have the maximum degree of self-sufficiency in food and energy production. An obvious strategy would be to create businesses related to these two areas. Thus the idea of a venture capital company arose—a company that would invest only in sustainable, environmentally friendly products and production methods, and particularly in businesses where a physical location at or near an ecovillage was possible. This meant they had to be human scale, decentralized businesses.

I liked this concept for another reason. Prudence dictated that Gaia Trust could only give away a limited amount of its total assets in any one year as grants. The major part of its assets that were not tied up in Gaiacorp would have to be invested in something. Why not in something directly related to its grants program in order to get the maximum leverage of its funds. Thus the concept of Gaia Technologies—a green venture capital company—was born.

I pointed out to the others, who were not familiar with venture capital, that this "yang" strategy was very long term. The typical cycle for an investment is about seven years from first investment to maturity. Jobs would not likely be created in ecovillages the first ten years. Gaia Tech would rather be a parallel development that would hopefully converge with the "yin" strategy in the long term.

9

Green Technologies

Developing a strategy for Gaia Technologies A/S, or Gaia Tech, as we called it, was greatly dependent on the funds available from Gaiacorp, which had a very volatile and uncertain income, very much dependent on its performance in the currency markets. The early years went very well. The later years not so well. In the Fall of 1991 the outlook was very good. The nature of Gaiacorp's business strategy required that the lion's share of its capital was tied up in the business. I estimated that roughly 10% of total capital could be made available each year to Gaia Trust activities, including Gaia Tech. That meant something like order of magnitude $1 million per annum available for operations and investments of Gaia Tech. That is not very much capital in the venture capital business. One consequence was that we would have to limit ourselves to our domestic Danish market. This conclusion was also dictated by the limited human resources that we could allocate to the project within those budgetary constraints.

We identified a number of key areas where it made sense to seek out companies that might in time provide sustainable jobs in ecovillages: energy, food, education, alternative banking, communication, consulting, health, and ecological building. Projects would have to be environmental friendly, including both end product and production technology, they would have to be commercially viable, making some profit, and they would have to be small-scale, suitable for job creation in small communities.

I envisaged Gaia Tech eventually having three areas of expertise, appropriate technology, professional management, and merchant banking. I imagined that if we were successful, at some point we could attract outside capital to manage, for example from the pension funds, just as Gaiacorp had done. In fact I envisaged from the start that Gaiacorp would eventually be sold off and all our resources concentrated on our two-pronged yin-yang activities in Gaia Villages and Gaia Tech at a much higher level of activity. Gaia Tech might then become a kind of international green conglomerate working closely with the global ecovillage movement.

That was the dream. The reality turned out quite differently.

The initial strategy was similar to Gaia Villages. We first commissioned a survey of the field by a UK consulting group associated with E.F. Schumacher's ideas ("Small is Beautiful")[1], then held a brainstorming seminar with key people in Denmark. What we found was that the field was very immature, very embryonic, and filled with a lot of interesting ideas and commercially unproved prototypes. There was no end to the list of people who were convinced they had the solution to an important problem, be it integrated fish farming, waste water treatment, a new windmill type, an environmentally friendly solar cell, or an organic food product. You name it, and there would be twenty proposals on the table, all requiring financing for prototype development. The number of companies with an actual product with a track record was very few. And those that had often were sufficiently mature that they could get all the traditional bank financing they wished, for example the big windmill companies. This was rather frustrating for people like myself coming from a business school background that had focused more on the problems of established companies.

We had neither the human resources nor the finances to enter the minefield of prototype development. No matter how good an idea may sound, it is a long way from a good idea to the marketplace. Most of the entrepreneurs we ran into had no idea how to run a business. They seemed to think that having the concept was the most important thing, and completely underestimated the importance of cost control, liquidity planning, marketing analysis, management structure, sales forecasting, the whole gamut of running a viable business. So we found that the number of realistic opportunities available was actually quite limited, to some extent confirming the traditional venture capital mantra that says there is no lack of capital, only a lack of good projects.

This points up an interesting problem. Politicians who talk about the need to create more jobs do not seem to understand what is really needed. Their plans always seem to assume that the problem is a lack of capital investment. But it is really more a question of how to finance these "idea men" in the early stages of prototype development. Neither venture capital firms nor banks will touch them due to the high risk of failure. Even a very sympathetic firm like Gaia Tech has to keep away. The only thing a budding entrepreneur can do is to mortgage his house, get a few loans from his family and friends, and start up in a garage, saddled with incredible bureaucracy and costly paper work, and the same basic reporting requirements as established companies. Not surprisingly, most of them fail under these circumstances. The ones who do succeed often find that once they get to the point where they are making money, the banks and venture capital firms begin to show an interest, just when they are not needed anymore.

As we were the only firm in this particular niche in Denmark, the word got around quickly, and we began receiving a continuous stream of proposals, most of them not very realistic. But small companies cost just as much to process as larger companies, which, of course, is one reason why most venture capital firms stay away from small firms. In time, we did find what seemed like a few reasonable investments for Gaia Tech, and in several branches: organic fast food, solar cells, publishing, organic cheese production, organic corn flakes, organic dry goods, small windmill production, an alternative bank, and organic meat production. We also reserved a small pool of "mad money" for projects that were not particularly viable commercially, but were creating jobs at one of the Danish ecovillages, and had four or five such cases.

We deviated about five times from our normal principle of requiring at least a prototype before committing funds, and took the chance because the technology looked so promising. In every single case, we were wrong to go in too early, and had to stop the bleeding at some point, just confirming that the principle of no prototype financing was the right one.

In the investments we did make, the general experience can be pretty much summed up by what we came to call "Kjeldsen's Law" after Lars Kjeldsen, the chairman of the Gaia Tech board. Kjeldsen's Law says that to get a realistic projection of cash flow from a budget presented by an applicant for funding, you should (1) multiply his cost estimates by three (2) divide his income estimates by two.

We severely overestimated the ability of the project initiators to make realistic cash flow estimates. We were simply too naïve. Their optimism was typically just overwhelming, based on wishful thinking and with no margin for error. But this was often difficult for us to see. Typically the historical accounts were either nonexistent or too short-lived to be a useful guide. Sometimes the entrepreneur lied to us or withheld information that would have affected our decision. The result was a continual need to make tough decisions, either put in more cash or let the company go broke. We were continually having a knife put to our throats.

We severely underestimated how much assistance these companies needed in even the most elementary management techniques, like for instance producing monthly accounts. Just getting reliable sales figures in several cases was a major task.

We also made the naïve assumption that the people we were dealing with were being honest with us. But something seems to happen to some people when the going gets tough. We had three separate cases of being given incorrect manipulated sales figures by the manager in order to paint a rosier picture than the reality. One of our managers in desperation manufactured false invoices to get additional bank loans, and illegally held back funds due the tax department. He was the subject of a police report after being fired. Another channeled company funds into his privately-owned company, made illegal loans to himself, and put his wife on the payroll, all in flagrant disregard of his contract, besides which he fed us false sales figures. He was of course fired also. A third case fed us incorrect sales figures, entered into a contract without the board's knowledge that could have bankrupted the company, and almost did, and deliberately misled us on the state of the company, all in order to justify more funds from us to keep him afloat. But often it takes time and a lot of money to find out that you are being conned.

Of course, we had our successes too. In every case of success we noted that we were dealing with a man or woman of integrity and honesty. But the few successes were not enough to outweigh the failures. Financially, Gaia Tech has been a big loss-maker to date. The final chapter has yet to be written. However, its future is going to be far more modest than I had hoped initially, partly because far less capital is available now than in the early days due to financial setbacks in Gaiacorp, which has had a rocky period in the last few years. We must now consider whether the Gaia Trust strategy should be revised, as the benefits accruing to the ecovillage movement have been minimal, and there are few signs of that changing in the near future.

On balance Gaia Tech has been a mixed experience. The bottom line results have not been good. Perhaps it is still too early for the concept to succeed. As usual, it is difficult being a pioneer. I believe the basic concept is sound and will eventually succeed in a big way, possibly in America, where I suspect it would be easier. But there have been some positive aspects too. Almost everyone who has been in touch with the project has lauded its goals, even businessmen from the establishment.

A few pension funds have expressed an interest in what we are doing and in possible participation in our investments. But there is a curious mentality at work here that more often than not prevents any action from being taken. At the annual meetings, many vocal members of pension funds typically stand up and demand that their fund should be more green and more ethical in its investment policies, and not just look at financial return. A board is elected with this mandate. A few such boards have contacted us for advice on how to implement a "green" strategy. But something happens once the board is elected and they have to make hard decisions. There is always someone who says "What if it goes wrong? We will be criticized." Or "We have to go for maximum return. We are not a charity. We may even be breaking the law if we don't." The board quickly becomes very conservative. Ironically, this is just as true for union funds as for any other. They quickly become conservative capitalists. They just don't have the backbone to follow their members' wishes and take a few chances. They are administrators, not entrepreneurs.

When one such union fund with several hundred million in investments asked me for advice, I suggested they switch $300,000 of their short term cash deposits to Mercury Bank, the alternative bank we were backing. Here they could even get a slightly better rate than their current bank was paying, and they could be sure that the funds were being used for good, ecological projects. Mercury Bank even had a record of a lower percentage of bad loans than all the major banks, who had all lost big time in the 1990s on risky real estate loans and by backing dubious tax and speculative schemes that Mercury Bank would never touch. Nevertheless, the board of the pension fund ruled that it was *too risky* to put that much of their funds in a bank with a net worth of only 12 million. "What if the bank failed?" they asked. Gaia Trust, with a much more modest capital, had no trouble finding over $600,000 to put into Mercury's capital base plus additional funds on deposit, because we were convinced that it was good for society as a whole to promote ecology and sustainability. That is the difference in mentality we were up against. I am certain that if the members of the pension funds were polled individually, they would do the same as we do, and take a few chances.

There have been some positive developments in the general area of raising the consciousness of businessmen in this period also. For example, several organizations of businessmen have been formed internationally in recent years to encourage socially responsible investment, ethical accounting, and the like. One of the first was the Social Venture Network (SVN) in the US. I happened to know one of the initiators, Josh Mailman from New York. He took the initiative in getting a similar European organization started in the autumn of 1993 and suggested

I help. Gaia Trust subsequently became one of the founding members of SVN Europe, which now has several hundred members and contacts to a network of over 2000 businesses internationally. Part of their mission statement says:

> *We are a network of socially and environmentally engaged entrepreneurs and business leaders, dedicated to changing the way we and the world do business. Our goal is to integrate the values of a socially and economically sustainable society into day to day business practices.*

We have also seen during this period evolution of the concept of "green accounting" in Scandinavia, particularly in Sweden, and "ethical accounting" in Denmark, which have engaged a large number of leading corporations in the region, not least due to my old partner Peter Pruzan, who has been a pioneer in this area at the Copenhagen Business School. These are all encouraging signs that businessmen are beginning to realize that they have a social responsibility.

Many young people especially have told us of the great inspiration the Gaia Tech initiative has given them. After a TV program on Gaia Tech was aired, we were approached by a number of dissatisfied "establishment people" looking for more meaningful jobs. One, from a major Danish bank, reported that the program had made a great impression on his colleagues. He decided on the spot to leave the bank and join Mercury Bank at a lower salary. Hopefully our efforts have not been a waste. Perhaps our experiences will in the least help others to avoid our mistakes.

10

The Global Ecovillage Network

Gaia Trust received the Gilmans' ecovillage report in the spring of 1991.[1] We discovered in this way many very exciting and very different projects around the world, with a heavy emphasis on North America. However, it struck us that none were ideal, replicable models for the 21st century sustainable society. We had imagined that things had developed further than they had. It was clear that the whole process was still in its embryonic stage.

As the next step, we and the Gilmans invited a small number of the best existing ecovillages along with a few leading thinkers on sustainabilty issues, including former adviser to the US Agency for International Development David Korten[2] and the charismatic Swedish doctor Karl-Henrik Robert, who started *The Natural Step* movement, to a five day brainstorming meeting in September 1991 in Denmark, about twenty people in all. This meeting taught us the vital importance of networking among the geographically dispersed experiments across the globe. New projects and cross-linkages were established between people who had not known each other before, but found that they had common ground on which to enthusiastically work together. Many new projects and ideas evolved from those few days, many of them after the participants went home. It became clear that forging links was vital to the success of any global strategy. By linking, we learn from each others successes and failures and strengthen the overall movement towards sustainability.

At the same time, it became clear to us that Denmark was somewhat ahead of many other countries in developing the ecovillage concept, perhaps because of twenty years of experience with cohousing, which had been quite successful, but limited in scope. Many Danes were now looking for a broader vision that went a step further. A number of ecovillage projects were already underway—about fifteen or so, most very embryonic, but three that were well established.

So the next step we took was to help the Danish ecovillage projects get organized into the Danish Ecovillage Association, which turned out to be a very effective way to strengthen the movement, not least through lobbying activities.

A major problem that was slowing the growth of the movement was the lack of financial support. In 1993, we asked the ecovillages we had contact with what their major needs were, and found that the number one factor restricting growth was money to build infrastructure and homes. A lot of money was needed. The requirements were orders of magnitude larger than what Gaia Trust could provide. Gaia Trust had to focus its limited resources on networking, communications, and meetings. The amounts available for individual projects was minimal.

We began to think in terms of establishing a dialogue with other funders. So I decided to go to the annual meeting of the Environmental Grantmakers Association (EGA) in Bretton Woods, New Hampshire, in October, 1994, to sound out the American foundations. The EGA is a subset of the American foundations that each have an active environmental program as part of their policy objectives. My original idea was to form an international foundation that would support the further development of the ecovillage movement. However, I was in for some surprises that forced me to rethink the entire strategy.

My first surprise was how little international support was coming out of the USA from the EGA. Almost 80% of the foundations had restrictions in their charters that limited them to funding American projects only. Those that did some international funding often had a narrow regional or sector program. That pretty much scuttled the idea of an international foundation.

A second observation was that they were in a period of crisis. They were being criticized and obviously hurt by the Wise Use movement— a right-wing property-rights movement, which accused the environmental movement of being out of touch with the common man, sitting in their ivory towers at the academic institutions. The Wise Use movement had taken over the environmentalists' grass roots organizing talents and were "kicking our ass," as Dave Foreman (founder of Earth First!) bluntly put it. In truth, I had to agree with some of the criticism. They badly needed a new, more positive, vision.

I felt that support for the ecovillage movement would be an ideal response, and said so at every opportunity. It could promote a positive vision of sustainability that was very much on-the-ground, and provide an effective counterattack that was not just a defensive move, but put forth a new vision. But the idea met with very little understanding or sympathy, a response that I have since met many times from people working in the traditional funding environment of foundations, governments, World Bank, etc. They do not yet appreciate the potential for real change in this movement. Mainstream funders tend to think top-down, large scale, and sectorially, where our strategy is a more holistic, bottom-up, organic approach. There is a clear clash of cultures and approaches here.

My experience is that you get the most bang for the buck supporting, with small amounts of money, people who have already demonstrated an ability to complete a successful, small project. Then let the amounts grow as the person grows. I have also observed that the best money is often given to support meetings between people, for networking. Many of the best people working on the ground can simply not afford to travel. But this point does not seem to register with many funders. Their traditional approach shuns both of these lessons. Several of the EGA members said it was directly against their policy to support meetings. Ironically, the one foundation officer that supported my view was also the only one that was a former grass roots activist. She agreed that financing meetings was the single most important thing for the grass roots.

My final surprise was the lack of coordination between the grant-making activities and the investment activities in the American foundations. Except in the very smallest foundations, the two functions were managed completely separately, often in different cities. I pointed out that their investments were often supporting the very things that their environmental grants were fighting against—much the same argument as we used in the Rainbow Bank project. I outlined our policy in Gaia Trust which was to invest, through subsidiary Gaia Tech, in companies that were supporting the same vision as the grantmaking activity. If they allocated just 10% of their investments in the same way, it could have a tremendous impact, as their investments funds are in the trillions of dollars. There was very limited understanding of this argument also, as it went against the grain of their traditional way of thinking. There was, however, a small minority that was thinking along similar lines and intended to push the issue to the forefront of their future agenda.

The one positive result of this visit was the view expressed by several program officers that it would be more fruitful to establish a dialogue with an association of ecovillages than to receive proposals from individual projects. And that the EGA member involved should be an active partner in formulating projects. Thus it was that upon my return, we dropped all ideas about forming an international foundation, and decided instead to focus on establishing regional networks that could enter dialogues with the establishment, fundraise together, and lobby for new legislation. The Danish experience confirmed to us that this was a viable strategy.

Thus began the gradual evolution of the concept of an international network of regional networks linking them, in what came to be known later as GEN (rhymes with "when")—the Global Ecovillage Network.

The initial GEN "seed group," which was quite diverse in make-up, history, and state of evolution, consisted of the following: Findhorn Community, Scotland; The Farm, Tennessee, USA; Lebensgarten, Steyerberg, Germany; Crystal Waters, Australia; Ecoville, St. Petersburg, Russia; Gyürüfü, Hungary; The Ladakh Project, India; The Manitou Institute, Colorado, USA; and The Danish Ecovillage Association. These were chosen for a variety of reasons, including geographical spread, attractiveness as models, and personal contacts. None were considered perfect models, but all had something vital to contribute.

A major watershed in the development of GEN occurred in October 1995 when Findhorn, assisted by GEN and Gaia Trust, held a conference on "Ecovillages and Sustainable Communities," which was a great success attended by over 400 people from 40 countries. Over 300 had to be turned away. The interest in the concept was immense. We decided to establish three regional networks covering the globe geographically, with administrative centers at The Farm, Lebensgarten, and Crystal Waters. Gaia Trust committed to covering expenses to support the networks for 3-5 years, and to act as coordinating secretariat out of its Gaia Villages office in Denmark. Interested ecovillages, as well as individuals and other interested parties were encouraged to join the regional networks which all have an open-ended, democratic, non-hierarchical self-organizing organizational form. As the organization grows, it was envisaged that the three initial regions will split into several autonomous regions.

Since the Findhorn conference, the Western Hemisphere has been divided into eight sub-regions, the Asian network in two, and over twenty national networks are active in Europe.

In order to maintain the integrity of the original vision within a structure that is open for anyone to join, GEN developed the concept of an ecovillage audit to measure the degree of attainment of any particular project on a multidimensional scale. This model—which is now accessible on the GEN Internet site, enable the networks to define "qualified" ecovillages as those that have come furthest in their development. Organizationally, it was intended that representatives of "qualified" ecovillages will have voting rights, while "initiatives" and other interested parties could be associate members. Besides preserving the integrity of the vision, this approach gives every project a yardstick to see how close it is to the ideal, and thus where it can improve. Of equal importance, the structure means that anyone can join their region's network, linking in to the nearest node anywhere across the globe. The hope is that with sufficient support, the network can evolve into an instrument of real change. All who support the vision are encouraged to consider joining. Terms of membership and services provided are evolving in real time. It can all be followed on the Internet.

The Internet was a technology that hit the scene at just the right time for GEN. The Net is ideal for a thinly dispersed global network. A GEN information data base has now been established on the Internet and is expanding quickly, having over 2000 pages by the spring of 2000.[3] The site was getting about 700,000 'hits' per month at this time, and has links to many other organizations and data sources. The site now includes profiles of a number of ecovillages who wish to present themselves to the world, resource lists for special skills, lists of relevant books and videos, a calendar of events, a complete listing by region of existing ecovillages and chat groups on financing, permaculture, ecological building, etc. Future plans include fundraising facilities with multiple choices for donors, e-commerce for "green products" across the globe, a 'classified ad' service, ecovillage tourism, and a global clearinghouse for complementary local money systems. As mentioned, everyone is welcome to join the GEN regional networks without conditions. This include ecovillage projects, of course, but also individuals and organizations that have an interest in what is happening.

Our work with many different types of projects in GEN led us to make certain general observations. Ecovillages tend to fall into three motivational categories: ecological, spiritual, and social. Each of the three groups is working on a positive alternative vision, reacting to what it perceives as a major deficiency in current mainstream society.

The ecologically motivated are reacting to environmentally unsustainable policies, and tend to emphasize living in harmony with nature, permaculture, and self-reliance in food production and energy.

The spiritually motivated are reacting to the spiritually barren philosophy of Western materialism and what they perceive as dogmatic narrow-mindedness of many traditional religions. They tend to emphasize taking responsibility for their own lives and personal development.

The socially motivated are reacting to the alienation of the individual due to institutionalization of traditional support functions, the breakdown of the family, and the marginalization of the weaker members of society. They tend to emphasize re-establishing "community," and are closely associated with the cohousing movement. The latter is closest to the mainstream and represents the easiest first step for many. All three groups often include citizens actively promoting Agenda 21, Global Action Plan, Natural Step, Voluntary Simplicity, and similar grass roots initiatives.

These categorizations are not clear cut. Many ecovillage communities have all three aspects represented. As they learn from each other, there seems to be a tendency to widen horizons, as they integrate each other's values and experiences, and expand their visions.

A very important aspect of the ecovillage movement that cannot be overestimated is that it follows a positive strategy, and is not a negative protest movement. Many GEN members, who were former environmental activists, have emphasized how big a difference it makes for their empowerment and personal satisfaction to be *for* something instead of *against* something. I always emphasize that we are all part of the problem, and must all be part of the solution. No one can be left out. There is no "us" and "them" as in many protest movements. And no missionaries. Just quiet builders of a new vision.

After the Findhorn meeting, our thoughts in GEN began to focus on the next big event, the UN Habitat II conference coming up in Istanbul in June 1996. We began to see this as an opportunity to put the GEN vision before the world as a concrete response to the global crisis. At the same time, we would make an appeal for funding the many people around the world who wanted so much to live according to Agenda 21, but were meeting all kinds of obstacles, including a lack of financial support from their governments.

Thus arose the idea for GEN and Gaia Trust (because an accredited NGO was necessary—GEN was not yet a legal entity) to put forward a proposal to the UN in Istanbul for a 100 million dollar fund to build 50 ecovillages across the globe as examples of Agenda 21 and as teaching centers for their regions.

Gaia Trust was one of the few NGOs that were given permission to speak directly to the official delegates at the conference. This was no doubt due to the fact that GEN was generally acknowledged to have had the best and largest NGO presence in Istanbul with an exhibit covering over 150 square meters, 20 representatives from ecovillages around the world manning the floor—many of them leaders in their professional fields, and with a separate program of 40 workshops on sustainable habitats. The exhibit also included a specially constructed straw bale wall hung with professional quality presentations of several GEN member communities, a live Internet connection, several ongoing videos, a windmill, a solar cell demonstration, running water, games to play, and best of all, dancing for all comers every day at 3:00 p.m. led by Irish/German Declan Kennedy, the first GEN Chairman, who happened to be a professional dancer in his young days. It was a great hit with the public.

In Istanbul, GEN was formally incorporated as an association of autonomous regional networks, three initially as outlined in the previous chapter. This UN conference was also the first occasion at which GEN presented itself publicly. The response from other NGOs and official delegations was uniformly positive. Many saw GEN as one of the few examples of an organization that not only had a strategy for global change, but was actually carrying it out on the ground.

A big attraction was the artistic and beautiful special report entitled "The Earth is Our Habitat,"[1] which presented the proposal to the UN, and was largely Hildur's work. GEN called it "A vision with the power to change the world." And it was received very positively by everyone, including the Secretary General Wally N'Dow.

Since the Istanbul meeting, the proposal has been circulated in a number of places. It was mentioned in Wally N'Dow's report to the General Assembly. GEN has taken it to the Rio+5 meeting, to the UNEP, and to the Nairobi UN headquarters for Human Settlements. Incredibly, it seems to fall between the cracks. In spite of a lot of sympathy, there does not seem to be any place in the UN bureaucracy where an altruistic proposal of a global nature like this fits, and it will probably never be realized, unless one or more countries will take up the initiative and offer to sponsor it. I cannot imagine any single use of funds that would have more leverage in moving the planet toward sustainability. Meanwhile, billions are being spent as usual on traditional prestige projects, on industrial marketing disguised as foreign aid, and the insatiable military. No wonder we are in trouble.

11

A New Culture Emerges

It was in the late spring of 1992 that the thought first occurred to me that something fundamental in our society had shifted. There were a dozen of us having lunch together outside on a sunny May day, discussing the upcoming Danish referendum on the Maastricht Treaty, which would launch the European Union. I expected to see a landslide victory for the "Yes" side, but to my great surprise, a straw poll of those present indicated that not one, including myself, was going to vote "Yes." This was in spite of the fact that those present were a very mixed group, representing the entire political spectrum.

After the fall of the Berlin wall in 1989, leading European politicians and the European Commission saw the opportunity for a bold initiative that they thought would pave the way for a peaceful, united Europe. The Maastricht Treaty proposal was hastily drafted and launched without much debate. In Denmark, one of the few European Community countries that required a referendum, and a country with a long tradition for debate and voter participation, a surprise was in store. In spite of massive campaigning for a "Yes" by all the major political parties and all the media, the Danish people rejected the Maastricht Treaty just a few days after our luncheon This sent a shock wave through Europe, as unanimity was required to adopt the proposal.

The Danes action was not only completely unexpected, it was the subject of much misunderstanding, both within and outside of Denmark. Why was Denmark "rejecting" Europe? Was Denmark against peace in Europe? Had the Danish politicians not explained the situation clearly enough? Were the Danes Isolationist? Nationalistic? Why, when everyone else in Europe could only see the advantages of further integration, were the Danes marching to a different drummer?

In my opinion, all of the above reasons for the "No" given by the commentators were well off the mark. Neither the foreign commentators nor the Danish politicians seemed to understand what was going on. I thought there was an interesting story here that would also be of interest outside of Denmark, and might affect the voting on Maastricht in other countries. It was for this reason that I took the initiative in quickly producing a book about why the Danes said "No" to Maastricht—*When No Means Yes; Danish Visions of a Different Europe,* which was published in Danish, English, and Spanish, and partially translated into French.[1] It was an anthology with contributions from 17 different persons, who outlined their reasons for rejecting Maastricht, which were many and varied.

Most of the book's contributors were not opposed to membership in the European Community, and all were very much in favor of international cooperation. However, many of them felt that a less centralized, more democratic form of cooperation would be preferable, and indeed necessary as the number of members increased, especially as the cultural diversity would be so much greater. It was emphasized, as reflected in the title, that the "No" was not a "No" to Europe, nor to international cooperation, but to this particular model, which was considered to be fatally flawed.

It is interesting that none of the other European Community members saw what Danes called the "democratic deficit" in Maastricht as a major problem. The illustrates clearly the differences between the Nordic countries and the countries south of the Danish border. In most of those countries, there was almost no public debate. Indeed, aside from France and Ireland, there was no opportunity for the voters to even vote on it in a referendum, in spite of the fact that they are formal democracies, and were ceding some of their sovereignty. The Danish definition of democracy is different from other places. It is not just a question of going to the ballot box every four years or so, but of ongoing participation in the political process at the local level, what the Danes call "Folkestyre." One of the Danes' greatest fears is to lose this tradition in the bureaucracy of a Maastricht-type European Union.

The Danish "No" was an example of what happens when politicians are out of touch with the people. Maastricht was from the beginning a top-down political project, not a wish of the European people based on *their* needs.

The Maastricht Treaty is now history. The Danish government refused to accept the will of the people, and eventually got approval for a modified version with four so-called "exceptions." Later again, a third referendum narrowly approved the marginally better Amsterdam Treaty in May, 1998.

Seen from the vantage point of year 2000, it occurs to me that what we may have seen in the Danish Maastricht vote in 1992 was a clash on a rather new global issue that had not previously been articulated as such. A new type of political schism was rearing its head for the first time, one that did not fit in with the traditional political party divisions, but one that will probably become more important in the coming years, not only in Denmark, but throughout the industrialized countries. We see here a strange situation where several political parties were split on the issue, and had large minorities, if not majorities, opposed to the leadership. And even more paradoxically, we had a situation where the parties of the extreme left and extreme right were fighting on the same side against Maastricht. What was going on?

I suspect we may have been witnessing the first clash between the forces of globalization and those of local community values, a clash which cuts across traditional party lines. "Local community values" is the term I use to represent a set of values that prizes and protects family, the environment, local community, culture, and local social networks, while money plays a secondary role. These are the typical values of ecovillagers, and of many others as well.

Possibly, a political movement may arise at some point which unites the people having these values. Many on the left oppose globalization because it strengthens the capitalistic transnational corporations (TNCs) while many on the right opposed it because they just want to be left alone to manage their affairs without interference from "big government," and especially not foreign bureaucrats. Then there is a third constituency—those who see the typical government priority of economic growth above environmental protection as a threat to the quality of their lives. The latter are found to different degrees in all parties, from right to left. Finally, we have a fourth constituency that prizes democratic participation in decisions at the local community level. Together, the four constituents represent about half the population in Denmark, as reflected in all the referenda on the EU, but only about 15% of the elected representatives, and they have little or no influence as they tend to be a minority in most parties except on the extreme left and extreme right. Thus the split between the globalization agenda of the mainstream political leaders and the "local community" agenda of half the population creates a potentially unstable political situation that may continue for some time, but not forever. Something has to give eventually.

The active supporters of local community values, who are not yet a single movement, have a much less confrontational strategy than the early environmental NGOs like Greenpeace and Earth First! For example, groups like the Global Ecovillage Network, Global Action Plan, the Sarvodaya movement in Sri Lanka, and the Voluntary Simplicity movement in the United States, whose members are quietly building an alternative culture through personal action rather than protest. Apparently they have a surprising number of "closet" supporters on the sidelines, as an interesting study by American sociologist Paul H. Ray suggests.[2]

Ray's study, carried out in the United States in 1996, indicates that something very significant is underway below the radar screens of the media. His method was to measure changes in social values and how they change over time. He identifies three major groups, which he calls "Heartlanders" (29%), "Moderns" (47%) and "Cultural Creatives" (24%). He describes them roughly as follows.

The Heartlanders are conservative, the religious right, provincial, characterized by rather rigid, dogmatic belief systems. They tend to reflect traditional small town values and attend the local church, and prefer TV to reading.

The Moderns are the dominant group—materialistic, egoistic, oriented towards consumption and success and the newest technologies. Their world view is rational "Newtonian."

The Cultural Creatives tend to value community, the environment, human values, are global in outlook, read extensively, watch less TV, are anti-authoritarian and reflect a "new consciousness" that is evolving. Sixty percent are women.

The most interesting aspect of Ray's study is that the latter group, which represents to a great degree what I have called "local community values," is the fastest growing group. It was hardly measurable in the mid-1970s, when it was less than 4%. Ray points out that we are observing here an almost explosive shift compared to known historical value shifts, which tend to happen rather slowly. The process to date, says Ray, has been unconscious, and may well accelerate when it becomes conscious.

A second interesting aspect of the phenomenon is that the Cultural Creatives have not yet found each other. They tend to feel isolated, and as yet have no common periodical, political representation, or common identity. This is due mostly to the fact that the media and the political process is controlled and dominated by the Moderns. However, that is now beginning to change with the Internet, where the Cultural Creatives are finding one another. I strongly suspect that the phenomenon Ray has observed is also present in Europe and elsewhere. I would guess that the percentage of Cultural Creatives in Denmark is even higher than in the USA.

In relation to Ray's terminology, it is clear that ecovillagers are part of the Cultural Creatives, comprising one of the front lines on this historical shift in values which is still in its early days. A confrontation with the Moderns, who are clearly supportive of commercial globalization, is inevitable sooner or later, in what may well be the major political conflict of the early 21st century—a conflict of value systems as the consequences of globalization become clearer.

12

Shareholder Protectionism

Let us look more closely at this great buzzword of the 1990s— "globalization." Few people have really understood what it is all about, and how much is at stake, because the media coverage has been willfully misleading. Firstly, the goals of globalization are diametrically opposed to those of the ecovillage movement. The two philosophies represent two vastly different value systems, which can lead to two very different future global societies, one in which everything is reduced to money, or one in which money considerations are subordinate to human values. The latter is what all the vast majority of Mankind wishes. The former is what they are about to get. In Paul Ray's terminology, the Moderns are in complete control at the moment, and the resistance from the Cultural Creatives is sporadic and barely on the radar, as they are far fewer and not yet organized into a true political force.

There is some confusion in the public mind caused by different uses of the word "globalization" by different commentators. I use the word in the sense of *commercial globalization,* which is the most usual usage. However, some use the word to cover a wide range of tendencies which link different parts of the world together, for example the Internet, information technology, cultural exchange, the global village, and so on. The distinction is critical because the latter tendencies are generally positive for Mankind as a whole, while the former, the commercial aspects, are of very doubtful value to the vast majority of people.

To its enthusiastic supporters, which include the entire private sector and most governments, globalization is the logical consequence of the triumph of "free market" capitalism over communism, of economic liberalism over "protectionism." Globalization is being sold to the world public with very clever PR by the TNCs and their political allies as a great benefactor of all Mankind. Inefficient and hitherto closed, "protected" markets are being opened up to competition, forcing prices down "for the benefit of consumers." A single global market for goods and services is the goal, with the unhindered flow of capital and goods across national borders as the enabling factor. The success to date of their strategy is epitomized in the WTO, the World Trade Organization, soon to be followed, they hope, by an even more ambitious project, the MAI—the Multilateral Agreement on Investments.

"Globalization" claims that it can deliver optimal resource allocation by removing the barriers to "free trade." Furthermore it promises sustainable growth, increased employment and a higher standard of living.

But what is the reality? In my opinion, "globalization" is not only based on a faulty theoretical foundation, it has not, cannot and will not deliver sustainable growth, increased employment, or higher standards of living—except for shareholders of the TNCs. On the contrary, I expect it will be a great disaster for humanity, both North and South. It will be stopped eventually, when the truth of its nature is revealed for all to see, but not before it has done tremendous damage.

Let us begin with the theoretical foundations. Economist Herman Daly points out the following:

"In neoclassical economics, the efficient allocation of resources depends on the counting and internalization of all costs. Costs are internalized if they are directly paid by those entities responsible for them—as when, for example, a manufacturer pays for the disposal of its factory wastes and raises its prices to cover that expense." [1]

But costs in the modern world are *not* internalized, because it has never been possible to reach international agreement on how to do it without losing your competitive position to another country that won't play along. The result is that we get a distorted use of resources that rewards those who exploit the situation by producing the wrong things at the wrong prices and are able to pass on the real costs of running their businesses to the general public.

The "free trade system" could more tellingly be called the "free ride system," because TNCs do not have to include in their product costs all the indirect costs they cause society, such as pollution of the land, sea and air, ozone holes, disappearing topsoil, exploding health costs, allergies, global warming, destruction of species, pesticides in food, antibiotic-resistant bacteria, crime, unemployment, escalating social costs, etc., etc. If they did, it would hardly be justified, as we often see today, to transport goods half way across the world and sell them below the cost of locally produced goods. Many of the most common, and most damaging products on the market, would never be manufactured if they were priced at their real costs to society as a whole. The road to success in global business today is to find a way to pass on as many of your costs as possible to the public, preferably to another country's public. The most profitable companies at this time are those that are most successful at getting someone else to pay the real costs of their doing business.

Another way of putting this is as follows. A fundamental axiom in Operations Research, which is valid for any optimization problem, is that proper resource allocation requires that benefits and costs must accrue to the same decision maker. Otherwise, you get distortion, i.e., the wrong solution, from a total point of view. And this kind of distortion is precisely what happens with the TNCs because of the failure to internalize costs. A corporation has many so-called "stakeholders"—i.e., people who have an intrinsic interest in the decisions made by the corporation. These include the shareholders, the employees, the customers, the suppliers, the government's Tax Department, and not least, the local community. However, "globalization" maximizes *only* the profits to the shareholders, while all the other stakeholders are left bearing the costs, for example, cleaning up the environment and dealing with unemployment when the corporation decides to move on to a more attractive, i.e., cheaper, location.

So while globalization maximizes the benefits to shareholders, and penalizes the other stakeholders, it is by no means clear whether there is any positive benefit at all in "free ride markets" to society as a whole. Indeed, there are indications that the marginal costs to the environment alone now exceed any benefits to the shareholders. "Globalization" should rightly be called *Shareholder Protectionism,* since that is really what it is all about. However, the clever use of "newspeak" by the TNCs, reminiscent of George Orwell's novel, "1984," sends the public a much different, positive sounding message. Unfortunately, both the public, and our politicians, have, under the powerful influence of the business community, taken globalization on board as their agenda for our common future.

Proponents of so-called "free markets" often justify their claims that their approach will satisfy the needs of all people with reference to the work of classical economist Adam Smith[2], but once again, their story line is faulty. It is true that Adam Smith showed that competition among many suppliers provides the lowest costs for the consumer. But what the "free riders" don't tell you is that one of Smith's most important assumptions was that capital remains *local.* When capital does not have a home, and when capital is concentrated in a few hands, the theory just doesn't work anymore. For example, we get the kind of sudden capital investment shifts that devastated Mexico a few years ago, and the Far East more recently. Indeed, Smith was opposed to monopolies and would without a doubt oppose "shareholder protectionism" if he were alive today.

A tragic irony of the current situation is that most governments, in spite of the lip service they give to promoting a sustainable future, e.g., at Rio in 1992, and more recently, at Kyoto in 1997, actually subsidize the very opposite, and with very significant amounts indeed. At a press conference at the UN in June, 1997, The Global Commission to Fund the United Nations, an independent international group brought together by American economist Hazel Henderson, documented that governments around the world, including signatories of Agenda 21, are subsidizing unsustainable development to the tune of $700 billion per year. For comparison, world governments at Rio in 1992 could only find $3 billion per year to promote sustainability, even though conference chairman Maurice Strong estimated that $100 billion per year for twenty years was necessary to do the job properly.

Governments the world over are misleading their citizens when making empty declarations at meetings like Rio in 1992 and Kyoto in 1997. This has been demonstrated for all to see by their failure to allocate more than a small fraction of the necessary funds requested for the clean-up at Rio, and by the subsequent failure to meet even the subminimal targets on CO_2 emissions since. They are close allies of the TNCs and have no intention whatsoever of making any real effort to tackle the issue of sustainability. They continue to think only of economic growth as the solution to all problems. But economic growth is an absolute dead end, as we will see below, and is the prime cause of the crisis in the first place.

Ironically, the public, when asked, invariably expresses the opposite priorities, as in a recent OECD survey. They want clean water, air and soil, safe food, a secure and peaceful environment, meaningful employment, and a pleasant, natural environment. And what are they getting? Polluted water not fit for drinking or bathing, air not fit for breathing, poisoned and disappearing topsoil, pesticides and antibiotics in their food, crime in the streets, growing unemployment, social fragmentation, and lots of platitudes about the need to clean up *when we can afford it*. But isn't it precisely "free ride" economics that is causing all these environmental problems in the first place?

The concept of unending economic growth as the solution to our problems is the conventional wisdom of our times, accepted without question by the whole spectrum of political parties in almost all countries, from left to right, and by the vast majority of the people as well.

But this does not make it true wisdom. On the contrary, it is classic denial. Refusal to recognize that things have changed forever. Our so-called "growth" is an illusion. It is a simple case of partying up while living off one's capital, in this case the finite raw materials and absorption characteristics of the planet. A civilization, like a spoiled playboy, can live high for a while. But then, at some point, the piper must be paid. That point is approaching very fast for us. It is only a question of time until things run out.

For true wisdom, we have to go to the indigenous peoples of this planet, people like Chief Seattle, who, in his famous speech to the victorious white man in 1854, said:

This we know: the Earth does not belong to man, man belongs to the earth. All things are connected like the blood that unites us all. Man did not weave the web of life, he is merely a strand in it. Whatever he does to the web, he does to himself.

Your destiny is a mystery to us. What will happen when the buffalo are all slaughtered? The wild horses tamed? What will happen when the secret corners of the forest are heavy with the scent of many men and the view of the ripe hills is blotted with talking wires? Where will the thicket be?
Gone!
Where will the eagle be?
Gone!
And what is to say goodbye to the swift pony and then hunt?
The end of living and the beginning of survival.[3]

Herman Daly points out the usefulness of what he calls "impossibility theorems" in science to save us wasting our energy pursuing unrealizable goals. In particular, he demonstrates "that it is impossible for the world economy to grow its way out of poverty and environmental degradation." Thus he shows that the very concept of the free market buzzword *sustainable growth* is an oxymoron—an internally inconsistent phrase. But all is not lost, he adds, if we focus on *development* rather than *growth*. As Daly puts it: "The economy must eventually stop growing but can continue to develop."[4] Development in this sense means qualitative improvements without material growth.

Daly goes on, citing a study by biologist P.M. Vitousek.[5] A clear limit to physical growth is that the human culture can obviously not consume more than 100% of the "net primary product of photosynthesis" provided by our sun. We are currently consuming about 25% of that total, and 40% of the more relevant land-based total. Thus a doubling of current total consumption would seem to be a realistic estimate of the maximum a mature, sustainable human society could expect, whatever the total population may become. For comparison, it would require a 7-doubling if everyone were to match the current level of American per capita consumption even at *current levels of population*. In the meantime, population is doubling every 40 years or so. For comparison, the Brundtland Commission called for an expansion of the world economy by a factor of 5 to 10—completely off the charts if Vitousek and his colleagues are right. Daly suggests that even the present level of economic production is unsustainable, and I tend to agree with him. We have hardly begun to pay the costs of our past transgressions.

Due to the photosynthesis limit, it would seem that a reasonable estimate of the long run destiny of Earth's civilization may well be a total production stabilizing at something below a doubling of current total consumption. How will people react when the reality of no further physical growth sinks in? How will the pie be distributed when it stops growing? Will we see voluntary reductions in Western consumption in sympathy with the starving masses of the South? Will the elites of Europe and America open their doors to the starving immigrants from Africa and Mexico beating on their doors, not to mention their own poor and homeless? Hardly! Nothing in human history suggests such magnanimity.

More likely, we can expect a further polarization or the world community into a tiny rich elite walled in behind secure boundaries, with a mass of desperate poor living from hand to mouth on the outside, continuing the trend of the past half century. We can also expect an increase in terrorism from desperate have-nots. This scenario sounds much more likely, based on past history, and would be a nightmare for everyone, including the walled-in elite. What we can expect from a continuation of current trends is a de facto WTO/MAI shareholder world government—a world of very few rich, first class citizens living in luxury behind guarded walls, banking their capital gains and controlling everything, while a vast destitute majority scrapes by outside in a world of "social apartheid."

The question inevitably arises: How did this terrible situation come about? Who is to blame? It can be tempting to blame the business community, pointing out their narrow focus on short-term profits and their lack of social consciousness and ethics. This is a tempting, but inadequate explanation. The individual businessmen who are making the decisions that are destroying the ecosystem and our cultural heritage are not evil. They are, on the whole, nice, ordinary people. Many are outstanding citizens. I have worked with them personally for years, and count many of them among my friends. Many of them are aware of the negative consequences to society of their actions, but feel they are unable to act otherwise. We must remember that they do not make the rules by which they play. They have great influence, yes. But they do not make the laws. Therefore their defense is incredibly simple. They say they are hired to make the maximum profit for their shareholders while operating within the law. The effect on the rest of society is not their problem. This is a basic ground rule of "shareholder protectionism." Society cannot expect them to behave otherwise under the circumstances. If the CEO of a public company decides to take a different view, and joins, say, the Social Venture Network, and declares that from now on he will be socially responsible, the chances are 10 to 1 that he will be replaced by the shareholders with someone else, someone who will take on "shareholder value" as his mission.

Who does that leave as the responsible parties? Politicians? And hence those who elect them? Here the case is much better. It is, after all, politicians who have the power to change the laws. They could have internalized the indirect social and environmental costs to society decades ago. They could still bring the TNCs under control if they had the will to do it. Internalization is not a perfect solution, but it is enough to take back control of things and at least stop the worst effects of globalization. It is not easy, and requires a commitment to research and a will to do the job, but it is doable.

Then why haven't they done something? Why hasn't internalization even been tried? Why is there no research on the subject? Why isn't it even being discussed as a possibility? A politician who sympathized with the idea in principle would probably say in his defense that it is suicide for his country to do it alone, because the effect would simply be to make its products less competitive than the nations who would not go along. So why shoot yourself in the foot? Why waste money doing any research on it? He would also claim that he has very little power to make real change. Even US presidents have said the same. It is an all or nothing situation, he would say. It's either everybody in, or everybody for himself. So we find ourselves in this untenable dilemma. Since we have no institution of global governance on this planet, we get the worst possible result—uncontrollable globalization and environmental degradation until at some point the bubble will burst when the ecosystem can take no more.

Furthermore, a progressive but realistic politician would argue that political leadership cannot be too far ahead of the general populace without losing its mandate. And here he would have a good point. The general populace in the West has not yet understood the seriousness of the interlocking problems that are coming to a climax around the end of the millennium as we begin to meet the limits to growth on a finite planet. They are not prepared to make sacrifices for the less fortunate in far off countries or even for their own grandchildren. Indeed, many would argue that they are worse off than their parents, and quite so. Their mind set is still locked into the "new frontier" mentality of the industrial revolution. The Cultural Creatives are an exception, but are as yet a minority without influence. So we have here a genuine dilemma.

So the real cause of our dilemma is not so much any particular group, but rather the inability of our civilization as a whole to adjust in time to the demands of the shift from the phenomenally successful "new frontier" mentality that created the modern world to a "spaceship earth" mentality that explicitly recognizes the limits and demands of a finite planet. This is a mind-boggling jump, a paradigm shift of the first magnitude, one that requires us throwing out traditional ways of thinking about economic growth, reforming our institutions and our form of governance and radically reinventing ourselves. This is an event that occurs only once in the history of a dominant global civilization. We are right in the middle of it, and frankly, we are not able to handle it.

If politicians are right about their inability to do anything about it, then it would seem we have two possible outcomes. Either change will be brought about from below, by civil action, or we will have to go through the wringer before any real changes are made. The chances are very good that the latter will be the result. We will then have to go through a major financial and ecological collapse before making the necessary reforms. That route might be avoidable if either Europe or the USA had the courage to demonstrate true leadership by standing forth and declaring: "We will internalize environmental and social costs from now on in our products regardless of the consequences, because it is the right thing to do. Please join us for the sake of the planet."

I believe that the people of Europe might very well back that noble vision in the near future, if the alternatives were properly explained, and that others countries would follow the example. I am less optimistic about the USA, but would not rule out the possibility. I cannot envisage any other way that a collapse can be avoided, and even that may not be enough. It was my hope in 1992 that the Danish "No" to Maastricht would lead to a reconsideration of the whole European Union project that might have led to such a decision, one that was more in line with what the people wanted, one that would have put the environment solidly ahead of commercial considerations and in tune with the needs of the twenty first century. But that was not to be.

To be effective, internalization of costs requires a broad consensus, serious research, and a long term commitment. For example, industry should be given time to retool and develop new methods of production by introducing the taxes gradually over a period of ten years or more. Then it is entirely up to them if they survive or not. This type of approach would attract support from industry and their political allies on the right. Holland has had considerable success with this approach ("The Green Plan"), where industry was part of the solution, and not just a target for tax revenues.

It is inexcusable that governments have done so little to level the playing field in the most obvious area of all—organic food production. The people are crying out for clean food and drinkable water free of the pesticides, allergy-causing additives, genetic manipulation, growth hormones, salmonella and other bacteria that are a direct consequence of state-supported chemical farming and too-intensive farming practices. In spite of the enormous indirect costs these policies cost society, in the form of subsidies, environmental clean-up, increasing health costs, and research, not to mention the lower quality of life of both humans and animals, organic products are charged the same VAT (Value Added Tax) as traditional farm products. A recent survey in Denmark indicated that roughly half the population would buy organic food if it were not more expensive than traditionally produced food. It doesn't take ten years of research to see that we should cut the VAT on organic foods to more accurately reflect the true costs to society of chemical farming. Any revenue loss would be more than made up by savings in health costs and a happier populace. It is interesting that the tremendous surge in the market for organic milk in Denmark from nothing to 20% over the last five years came not as a result of any government program, but because one supermarket chain cut the selling price of organic milk to match traditional milk prices. The response was phenomenal, initiating a switch to organic farming by thousands of farmers. My experience with farmers is that most would prefer to farm organically if it were commercially viable. The irony is that organic farming *is* more viable commercially than chemical farming, if we just did our cost accounting properly.

Can the emergence of "green accounting," "ethical investment," the Social Venture Network and other similar initiatives make a real difference in the behavior of the TNCs? I hope so. That is why I support SVN. Certainly many concerned persons are working within the TNC world to bring about change. But I suspect they are fighting a losing battle, in spite of the growing lip service to social responsibility and ethical accounting by many TNCs. I fear that in the great majority of commercial companies, these soft concepts are mostly a PR ploy to create goodwill, and will not have any material effect on the really important decisions. I hope I will be proven wrong. As a basis for governance, I see the TNC philosophy as fundamentally and irreparably flawed, based as it is upon commercial rather than human values.

In my opinion, globalization is a financial accident waiting to happen—in the form of a global meltdown. The only unknown is when. The basic problem can be understood by the following six aspects:

(1) the free unhindered flow of capital across the world
(2) the concentration of hundreds of billions of dollars in the hands of very few large funds looking for maximum short term return
(3) The lack of liquidity in many of the markets that are attracting this money
(4) the herd mentality of these investors
(5) market linkages
(6) A systemic need to increase the volume of speculative investments as opportunities for easy profits decrease.
Let us look at these five factors more closely.

(1) Free global capital flow is a completely new concept, only a few years old, never seen in previous times, and completely contrary to the ideas of classical economics. It is a concept designed to enrich the forces promoting globalization, which I call "shareholder protectionism," primarily the owners of the transnational corporations. A key concept is that no demands are made on investors. All the advantages accrue to the shareholders. All the problems accrue to everyone else.

(2) Specialization in the intricacies of international investment has resulted in available investment capital flowing to a relatively small number of enormous specialist firms, over 3000 so-called "hedge funds" that invest in "anything that moves" as well a number of gigantic equity funds and pension funds, mostly American, and a few very large international banks. They tend to think alike. They are all looking for the maximum short term return on their funds, wherever that may be. In practice, this means primarily looking for the most attractive equity markets anywhere in the world, and getting the "hot money" out when something better appears on the horizon. They have no loyalty to any country, to their employees, nor to the local communities where they operate, nor do they have any regard for the cultural traditions of their host countries, for the environment, nor to anything else besides money.

(3) These investors insist on free capital movement so they can extract their capital quickly when they see a more advantageous opportunity elsewhere. In theory. In practice, only the largest and most

liquid markets can absorb the kind of short term pressures on stock prices and currencies that can result from such a decision to suddenly pull out of a market. They tend to get in slowly and get out all at once. This is the crux of the problem. Furthermore, in a panic situation, even the largest markets, USA, Japan, and the new Euroland will probably not be able to handle the pressures of a sudden repatriation of funds.

(4) The herd mentality is a critical part of the problem also. A fundamental axiom of the managers of these mammoth funds is that you don't get fired for doing the same thing as everyone else. This becomes the single most important investment criterion—not expected return, not risk, but doing what everyone else is doing. We see it at work in the way they all herd into Mexico, then Russia, then China, then Brazil, then Korea, then Malaysia, etc., etc. We see it at work the way the US stock market reaches unrealistic heights because no big fund manager is silly enough to risk his job by going against the crowd, and all hope they will be among the first to get out when the panic selling starts. We see the problem on the front pages when they all try to rush out of some market at the same time. That is when the risk of meltdown comes nearer.

(5) It used to be a prudent dictum to diversify your equity holdings by investing in many different stock markets at the same time, because they were relatively independent. That was true in the good old days when I was advising these same fund managers—about 20 years ago, before the free capital flow regime of the 1990s took firm root. It is no longer true. Today all markets are closely linked, as anyone who follows the markets must have observed. They are now highly correlated. This has dramatically increased the risks of global equity investment.

(6) One of the effects of globalization is to decrease the buy/sell spreads in many markets due to the sophisticated arbitrage between markets made possible by the latest information technologies. This has the effect of transferring profits from inefficient local monopolies to the TNCs—not so good for the local financial community, not a bad thing for the small local businessman, and great for the TNC arbitrageurs, at least until the game becomes known to everyone. However, as arbitrage opportunities are eliminated one after one, where will this kind of speculative money go? The answer is that it will go to lower margin, more speculative, larger and riskier operations. And that is a recipe for disaster. Nasser Saber makes the interesting point that there is a *systemic* need for speculative capital to constantly increase in size in order

to maintain profit growth in an environment with falling spreads—
very much in line with the claims of Karl Marx, as he points out.[6]

We saw a prelude to the "hot money" phenomenon in Mexico in
1994. We saw it again in Asia in 1997-98, where Malaysia and Indonesia
were hardest hit. I believe it is inevitable that such a crisis, sooner or
later will lead to a total meltdown unless fundamental reforms of the
globalization paradigm are made. In a meltdown, everyone gets hurt,
including shareholders, as stock and bond markets crash across the
world. A meltdown means, in practice, very widespread bankruptcies
of many major companies and even nation states, and of course many
smaller companies and individuals as well. It may even mean issue of
a new currency in some countries. This will be followed by global
depression, and many countries reinstating foreign exchange and
investment controls, as Malaysia did in the 1997-98 crisis.

Are there any quick fixes to the problem then? Within the current
globalization paradigm, there are none—only the well-known "management by crisis" strategy—capital infusion in the latest victim by the
IMF, primarily to save the overextended Wall Street investment banks,
and secondarily to prevent a domino effect and total panic. This policy is like putting a finger in an under-dimensioned dike, and is obviously not sustainable. The current powers-that-be have really nothing
else to offer within their paradigm. This is why I say that globalization
is, historically speaking, likely to be a relatively short-lived phenomenon. How long will it last? Nobody knows. A possible guess would be
another 10-15 years, after a final last hurrah of cancerous growth before
we experience *The Last Crash*.

The Last Crash is my expression for the ultimate financial crisis
which will occur sooner or later when the global investment community finally realizes that growth has to cease on a finite planet, and the
game is over. I give them about ten to fifteen years to make this "aha"
discovery, but it could happen much sooner. After that crash, which
will in all likelihood occur simultaneously with a total meltdown, there
will be no recovery. There will still be stocks and bonds. There will still
be international trade, albeit at a much lower level. And there will still
be TNCs, but highly regulated ones. We will then move slowly into a
new paradigm, where sustainability and self sufficiency, rather than
economic growth, will be the central concepts, as we begin to manifest
what I call the "era of ecovillage." I will come back to that vision in a
later chapter.

Are there other solutions within the dominant paradigm to financial crises besides IMF rescues? One which has been bandied about
the last couple of years is the so-called "Tobin tax" on currency

transactions. In my opinion, it is not a viable solution, because it is based on some fundamental misunderstandings about how the financial markets work. Because it has many supporters, I will spend some time explaining why it won't solve the "hot money" problem.

The attraction to some observers of a tax on currency transactions is based on the turnover statistic of one trillion dollars per day in the currency markets—more than ten times the actual underlying trade and investment flows. The thinking is that even one per mil of that would represent a billion dollars a day. If at the same time such a tax could eliminate "non-productive" currency trading, would not currency volatilities be reduced and would not a currency tax make investors think twice before repatriating their investments?

It sounds too good to be true. And it is. Leave aside for the moment the usual objection that it would be impossible to get all the major nations to agree. Even if they could agree, the effect of such a tax would be disastrous and would have the opposite effect to all the above supposed beneficial expectations. To begin with, the 90% so-called "non-productive" trading between the banks and large corporations plays a vital and purely beneficial role, by creating liquidity, spreading the risk among many banks and corporations across the world, minimizing volatility, and reducing the buy/sell spreads to order of magnitude 0.05% for the business community for the major currencies, a little more for the less liquid currencies. This means that businessmen and investors can eliminate their currency risk at very low cost. The turnover statistics from the IBS (International Bank for Settlements) are rather meaningless because they are measuring the same underlying deal ricocheting around the market all day between the banks as the risk is atomized into many small parcels in what is actually a very efficient allocation process. The actual money being moved by all this "froth" is trivial and has nothing to do with the "hot money" problem as such. A tax, even one of 0.1% would triple the normal spread and thus be a major cost to the market makers. It would have the effect of immediately drying up interbank trading and hence liquidity and the efficient allocation process. Many banks would drop out of the market entirely, joining many who already have done the same in latter years as competition has increased and spreads narrowed. Market liquidity would be reduced to a small fraction of what it is today without any effect whatsoever on the "hot money" problem. The immediate effect would be to increase volatility and the buy/sell spreads many fold, as the banks passed on the tax to their corporate clients, making it more expensive for businessmen and investors to eliminate their currency risk.

The predictable result is that businessmen would be forced to be even more speculative than they are now, i.e., more exposed to currency swings. Also international trade volume would decline as it would be much more expensive to import and export, which could trigger a global recession or exacerbate an ongoing recession. Furthermore, currency volatilities would be greater than today, as liquidity is the second most important factor that affects volatility, the less the liquidity, the greater the volatility. This is, of course why central banks like to intervene on Friday afternoons and around Christmas time. Incidentally, the most important factor is new information. Also, the income projections would be only a small fraction of the estimated because of the drying up of volume. And it would be the businessmen of the world paying the tax, not the financial speculators who were the target.

But most important of all, a tax, even one much larger than in my example, would have no effect whatsoever on the fundamental problem we are trying to deal with—the repatriation of "hot money," because the amount of the tax is insignificant compared to the losses on the stock and currency markets in any real crisis. Just look at the recent experience of 1997-98, where the Russian stock market dropped 80% and the dollar/ruble rate almost tripled. Other markets in Asia had similar, though less drastic collapses when the "hot money" pulled out, but all were far greater than any tax could have stopped. Much as I sympathize with the motive of its supporters, my conclusion on the Tobin tax idea? Forget it.

A cynic might well ask if Gaiacorp is not itself a part of the problem being as it is a player, albeit very small, in the foreign currency market, and this question deserves a response. The answer is that Gaiacorp operates very differently from the big hedge funds, in that all positions are in the four or five major currencies, and it follows a fully systematic decision model. Gaiacorp never deals in the less liquid currencies at all, nor does it invest in equities. So Gaiacorp is not contributing in any way to the financial crisis, but is a participant in the creation of market liquidity.

The fundamental problem of "hot money" is not currency trading, but investment flows. Pressures on currencies are only a secondary effect of attempts by the TNCs, foreign *as well as domestic,* to suddenly pull their capital out of the country they see as becoming less attractive for one reason or another. The lack of liquidity, both in equity markets and the currency market, then triggers the crisis. An effective solution would be to put restrictions on capital movement, for example, on how quickly capital, once invested, could be withdrawn from a country. Such restrictions are, however, unacceptable to the shareholder protectionism lobby, which is the root of the problem, and why fundamental reforms are necessary.

The hypocritical forces of globalization call such restrictions "protectionist." The real question however is: *who has the best case for protection?* The shareholders of the world, representing a very small rich elite, or the local communities of the world, representing 99% of humanity. Why should their jobs, industries, infrastructure, culture, families, values, and environment be systematically destroyed in the name of protecting this rich elite from commercial losses? And yet that is precisely what is happening today. Until we reverse our thinking on this one issue, there will be no reform worthy of the name.

It is time we took issue with the media's self-serving propaganda, when they continually broadcast their masters' mantra that "free trade is good" and that "protectionism is bad" for society. This is nonsense, and serves only one purpose, to package the TNCs exploitive agenda in a false halo, so they can go about their destructive business in a cloak of righteousness. Of course local cultures have every right to protect themselves against foreign commercial interests whose only motive is to extract as much money as possible from the local culture. Of course local cultures should decide who should be allowed to peddle goods in their territory, without having to provide "scientific proof" of anything. Of course local cultures should be the ones to decide under what conditions foreigners should be allowed to extract money from their society. These things ought to be obvious human rights, that cannot be magically reversed until they become—in the language of the globalizers, a "hindrance to free trade" (read: a hindrance to foreign commercial companies from extracting money from your local community). And yet this is precisely what the WTO (World Trade Organization) allows as it destroys local culture in the name of commercial profit to foreigners—turning life into death in what David Korten calls a pathological process akin to cancer in the human body.[7]

Supporters of globalization often claim that the protectionism of the 1930s was the cause of the Great Depression and must not be allowed to happen again. Therefore we need "free ride economics." But their history is faulty, as pointed out by Lang and Hines.[8] The depression was well underway before protectionist measures, such as tariffs on imports and currency depreciations, were taken. They point out that the prime cause of the 1930s depression was a combination of three things: the normal business cycle, a speculative stock market bust in 1929, and the subsequent failure of governments to undertake stimulative spending to promote demand for the products of industry. The protectionist policies were a response to the crisis, not a cause, just as in the case of Malaysia introducing foreign exchange controls in 1998.

Eventually we will live in a radically different society based on different values. One which is truly sustainable and humane. A society that will provide what *people* want, not what *shareholders* want. It is inevitable, and it is a future that a very small minority, including GEN— the Global Ecovillage Network—is preparing for now, whichever route we may take to get there. How we get there and how long it takes is the great uncertainty. Will we have a soft landing or a hard landing? Only time will tell. I will come back to that vision in a later chapter, including a scenario that could get us there from here. In the meantime, let us take a closer look at the TNC shareholders' plans to establish themselves as the new rulers of global society.

13

World Government: Phase 1

If you haven't heard of the WTO (World Trade Organization), it is because you weren't supposed to. "From start to finish, all elements of the negotiation, adoption, and implementation of the recent globalized 'free trade' agreements were designed to foreclose citizen participation."[1] Why? Because, my friend, if there had been citizen participation, it would never have been implemented.

"But why should I worry?," you may say. "It's just some technical trade document, right?" Wrong. It *looks* like a technical trade document. It was *sold* to politicians and the media as a simple trade document. But it is *not* a simple trade document. Here we have the spin doctors at work again, misleading us with their language. If there were truth in packaging, they should have called it "TNC World Government: Phase 1," but that would obviously have woken up a few people as to what was going on. The second nail in democracy's coffin is yet to be implemented, "TNC World Government: Phase 2," also known as the MAI—the Multilateral Agreement on Investments. More on that later.

In reality, the WTO is not about trade at all. It is a power grab. It has to do with institutionalizing "free ride economics" once and for all in order to protect TNC shareholders from environmentalists and other people who think there are other things of value to human society besides the profits of commercial companies. It also has to do with the transfer of sovereignty of nation states to the WTO, and how a three-man WTO team can dictate what laws your country may and may not pass in the future. *That's* why you weren't supposed to know.

Historically, the WTO emerged as a result of the "Uruguay Round" of GATT (General Agreement on Tariffs and Trade) trade negotiations as the new global agency to enforce the terms agreed upon in the late 1980s by over 100 countries. The fundamental provision is to allow any country to challenge any law in any other country as being a restriction to so-called "free trade." The TNC view, now conveniently incorporated in the WTO, is essentially that any attempt to pass on the indirect costs of their products to the TNCs themselves is a *restriction of trade*. Talk about turning the classical concept of efficient resource allocation on its head! But it gets even worse.

I wonder how many people could guess who has been rated "the most respected person in American" repeatedly in various national poles over the past several years, and why he is so respected? I can assure you he is not a politician. Nor would he be a candidate of the Fortune 500, nor of the media. Lawyer Ralph Nader is the man. He is the leader of a small group of dedicated environmentalists who do their homework thoroughly, and have been exposing the dirty laundry of the TNCs for three decades. Those surveys tell us a lot about the values of the average man-on-the-street in America, and give us a ray of hope for the future. Let's hear what he and his colleague Lori Wallach have to say about WTO—the World Trade Organization.

> *Approval of these agreements has institutionalized a global economic and political situation that places every government in a virtual hostage situation, at the mercy of a global financial and commercial system run by empowered corporations. This new system is not designed to promote the health and well-being of human beings, but to enhance the power of the world's largest corporations and financial institutions.[2]*

> *At risk is the very basis of democracy and accountable decision making that is the necessary undergirding of any citizen struggle for sustainable, adequate living standards and health, safety and environmental protection.[3]*

> *Trade agreements have moved beyond the traditional roles of setting quotas and tariffs and are instituting new and unprecedented controls over investment flows, innovations, public assets, and democratic governance.[4]*

> *The agreements promote the elimination of restrictions that protect people but increase protection for corporate interests.[5]*

> *Here is a sampling of targeted US laws: the Delaney Clause, which prohibits carcinogenic food additives; the Nuclear Non-Proliferation Act; the asbestos ban; driftnet fishing and whaling restrictions; the Consumer Nutritional and Education Labeling Act; state recycling laws; and limitations in lead in consumer products.[6]*

The chief negotiator of the USA for one of the preparatory meetings for the Rio conference estimated that as much as 80% of America's environmental legislation could be challenged and declared illegal before WTO panels.[7]

But it is not only American laws that are under attack. It is every country's laws that are at risk, with the TNCs as the only winners. Every country could make up a list similar to the American's. For example, American TNCs objected last year to EU restrictions on the banning of bovine growth hormones, which EU consumers feel are a potential health hazard. In this case, the tribunal ruled against the EU, infuriating many Europeans. This is just the beginning of a trend which is going to become much worse. The name of the game now is for countries to compete with each other in what Nader calls "a race to the bottom" to see who can offer the TNCs "the most miserable wages, the most lax pollution standards, and the lowest taxes," with the WTO three-man tribunal making the decisions. Nader sums it up in one word. "Neat." He adds, "Workers, consumers, and communities in all the countries lose, short-term profits soar, and the corporation 'wins.'"[8]

Let us look more closely at some of the provisions that will enable the TNCs to enforce their wishes on the nations of the world through the WTO.

1. The decisions of the three-man tribunal are final. There is no appeal. Furthermore, all documents and transcripts of the proceedings are secret. No media or citizen group can observe or comment. There is no required disclosure of possible conflict of interests of the panel members. While national government representatives are allowed to participate in the process, there is no mechanism to allow for opinions of other interested parties such as environmentalists, the medical profession, anthropologists, nor for human rights, labor, consumer or health activists. The only qualifications for panel members are legal training and previous experience as a foreign trade bureaucrat.

2. Under WTO rules, certain "objectives" are forbidden to all regional and national legislative bodies, including, for example, subsidies to promote energy conservation and sustainable farming practices.

3. The tribunal has the power to enforce sanctions on countries that refuse to remove laws that it, in its unilateral wisdom, considers WTO-illegal. Only unanimous opposition of all member countries can overrule a tribunal decision to impose sanctions—an impossible event in practice.

4. WTO rules are enforceable as concerns all existing and *future* laws of every member country. The WTO can challenge any law if the attainment of any WTO objective is being impeded, even laws that were never seen as trade-related.

5. The WTO is authorized to conduct ongoing negotiations on WTO
    provisions and to make binding decisions with a simple majority
    vote, leaving dissatisfied individual nations with no leverage to
    negotiate. The old GATT rules required unanimity.

Nader offers the comment that most people, including members of
the American Congress, probably find the above "unbelievable." It is
almost an invitation to the TNCs to take over as the first world government in a bloodless coup. People assume that their democratically
elected governments can impose whatever standards they want on
products that enter their marketplace without being second-guessed by
a biased panel of foreign trade bureaucrats in Geneva. But alas, they
are wrong. In effect, they have voluntarily sacrificed a vital part of their
sovereignty to the TNCs.

In this connection, Nader tells how he offered a prize of $10,000 to
a charity of his choice to any congressman who would sign an affidavit
that he had actually read the 500 page agreement, and could answer
ten simple questions about the contents. Only one congressman took
up the challenge, Republican Hank Brown of Colorado. After fulfilling
the conditions, he held a press conference, where he announced that
he was "aghast" at the contents, and was switching his vote from "yes"
to "no."

According to Nader, politicians in the USA as well as other countries, voted on the treaty without studying the contents. They relied on
the rosy descriptions of the paid corporate lobbyists. The advisers
swarming around the American Uruguay Round negotiations included
over *800 (eight hundred!)* business executives and consultants, but
only five representatives from environmental groups that were known
to be supportive or neutral, token labor representation, and no consumer rights or health representatives. Trade advisory committees on
timber, chemical, and other key environmental and consumer interests
had exclusively business representatives. It is no wonder that the TNCs
had a decisive influence on the result.

It appears that the text of recent trade documents was purposely
made complex, and publication delayed, and access made extremely
difficult, in order to cover up the real intent and to discourage real
debate. In the USA, the official NAFTA (North American Free Trade
Agreement) text appeared publicly only long after it had been approved
by the Bush administration and Bush had left office. According to Nader,
a Japanese translation of the WTO agreement appeared first *after*
approval—unread, in the Diet. A similar pattern was seen in many other
countries, who bought into the distorted views of their biased trade
advisors, and approved it without studying a translated copy.

Nader sums up resignedly: "It was little more than rubber-stamped by the very elected officials whose democratic powers it was designed to usurp."[9]

A question that is difficult to avoid is: why? Why, if the WTO/TNC power grab is as great a danger as described above, do all our politicians continue to assist them in achieving their agenda? Even the leftist parties that one might expect to oppose them are aiding them by buying into the myths of unending economic growth and globalization, Why do they make it so easy for the TNCs?

One answer is that the TNCs are very rich. They can afford tremendous lobbying task forces, as we saw above, and they can afford to "buy" a lot of politicians, both legally and illegally, especially in the Third World. In Europe, recent corruption scandals have rocked Italy, Belgium and France. Japan has had more than its share of corruption scandals recently, and a number of US politicians that were caught are currently serving jail sentences. A more subtle approach is through legal financial support and lobbying of politicians and civil servants, and through consultations with law makers, where we saw, for example, that there were 800 business representatives following the WTO negotiations in the USA. How many people were there to speak up for the case of strengthening local communities, which is far closer to the hearts of the American people? None!

A second answer is that they are also very clever. One way they are clever is not to use their powers too aggressively in the beginning. Their greatest fear is a backlash before they consolidate. So they proceed with caution as they gather power. We have hardly begun to see the consequences of the WTO yet, and can expect a slow acceleration. First we are to be lulled into a feeling of complacency. A second clever thing is their way of arguing about trade barriers. The business lobby in every country points out to their national politicians how many more exports they could sell if only the politicians would force their trading partners to open up their markets. Even leftist parties fall for this line. What the lobbyists don't tell you is that opening up markets is a two-edged sword, and with very high costs for the domestic economy.

And who pays the costs of the negative effects on your domestic market? Not the exporting TNCs. That's for sure. And certainly not the foreign TNCs that get access to your market. It is the domestic taxpayer that gets the bill. That means you, my friend, if you are still employed. It is the old story of the benefits and costs accruing to different players. The TNCs thrive, and you are paying the bills, as your local community's jobs, infrastructure, environment, and cultural traditions are gradually being destroyed by foreign commercial interests, while the tax base is being eroded—that means even higher taxes for you in the future. The costs are not reflected so much in the GNP as in the quality of your life.

A third answer is that the dynamics of globalization are complex and poorly understood by ordinary people, who are the victims, and by their elected representatives, who are not up to speed either. And even if the dynamics were understood better, ordinary folks cannot afford lobbyists, nor do they have the attention of the politicians, except at election time. The result is entirely predictable. We get things like the WTO and the NAFTA, and, coming soon, if all goes according to their plans, the MAI.

14

World Government: Phase 2

If you thought the previous chapter was hair-raising, fasten your seat belts for the sequel, because "Folks, you ain't seen nothing yet." I am talking about what the spin doctors call MAI—The Multilateral Agreement on Investments, and which I, based on the actual content, call *TNC World Government: Phase 2*. Before getting into the detail, let's hear what some very knowledgeable people have said about it:

> *The Multilateral Agreement on Investments is the most frightening proposition to face the Canadian people in my lifetime. If the MAI is implemented it will make it impossible to run our country our way, in our own interests, even if we wanted to. It has nothing to do with trade. It is about power and control. Power and control for multinational corporations and the international banks which finance them. It is a frightening scenario which forecasts a global economy in which nation states count for little—and ordinary voters count for nothing at all.*

Paul Hellyer, former senior cabinet minister, Canada; excerpts from his recent book *The Evil Empire: Globalization's Darker Side.* [1]

> *This could well be the most anti-democratic, anti-people, anti-community international agreement ever conceived by supposedly democratic governments.*

David Korten, Ph.D., former advisor for the US Agency for International Development, former Harvard University faculty, and Ford Foundation consultant, author of *"When Corporations Rule the World."* [2]

The MAI has generated uniform outrage among environmentalists world-wide. The MAI stands to transform governance around the world by literally replacing many roles now performed by governments with direct corporate rule. Unbelievably, the MAI would confer on private investors and corporations the same rights and legal standing as national governments to enforce the MAI's terms.

Lori Wallach, trade lawyer and director of Public Citizen's Global Trade Watch, Ralph Nader's organization. In testimony before the US House Committee on International Relations subcommittee of International Economic Policy and Trade, March 5, 1998.[3]

The MAI is a bill of rights and freedom for transnational corporations... a declaration of corporate rule.

Tony Clarke, Polaris Institute, and co-author of *The Multilateral Agreement on Investment and the Threat to American Freedom.*[4]

The MAI is the TNC's follow up to the WTO. Having tasted blood in their success with the WTO, they are now going for the jugular while on what they perceive as a roll. The secrecy surrounding MAI was such that even ministers of most governments did not know what was going on until almost two years after the secret talks began in early 1995 within the OECD. OECD bureaucrats and their TNC advisors worked on highly secret drafts of a new global power structure that would place all power in the hands of international investors, giving them unprecedented rights.[5] Why the OECD? After all, the OECD is normally seen as a source of trade statistics and reports, not a place to negotiate trade agreements. But it seems that the resistance of Third World countries to proposed investor protection clauses in the Uruguay Round negotiations were so vehement, that the TNCs decided to pull these clauses out of the WTO negotiations, and instead instigated the OECD talks behind closed doors. The plan was that once the OECD members—representing the 29 richest nations—signed off, then Third World nations would face an "offer they couldn't refuse": sign up or forego foreign investments, in classic Mafia style.

Apparently, the existence of the MAI first came into the public domain in early 1997 when the Clinton administration tried to slip it into the so-called "fast-track" bill that would circumvent normal legislative debate in the USA. It turns out the OECD/TNC conspirators were hoping to have it signed quietly internationally by April 1997 without any public debate—in what only can be described as a devious coup. However, after the text surfaced, reactions came strong and fast, not only from many outraged American Congressmen, who threw out "fast-track," but from abroad as well, particularly in France and Canada, who were soon leading a growing anti-MAI movement.

The outraged French Finance Minister described the MAI's corporate privileges to manipulate competition between countries as "blackmail" and declared that the French parliament would not sign. In Canada, half the provinces and numerous municipalities released statements against the MAI. The EU parliament passed a resolution rejecting MAI as "too far reaching." In New Zealand, the parliament was furious with its government when the story leaked. All over the world, NGOs are organizing. Efforts are being coordinated over the Internet, where most of the material for this chapter was obtained. To the chagrin of the initiators, the latest version of the rapidly changing text is readily available on the Internet. One current source is www.citizen.org. There are many others

So what is it that has provoked such passionate reactions to a socalled "trade treaty?" Let us look at some of the provisions in MAI that would cement the control, power, and not least, the wealth of the TNCs, if adopted.

1. Based on binding arbitration, the MAI would permit corporations to sue governments for compensation for limiting current or *possible future* TNC profits by passing laws such as environmental protection, human rights, labor standards, public health, consumer protection, and local community development, in short, any government policy or action that might limit their potential sales and profits.

2. Corporations could themselves choose the venue for the above binding arbitration, for example, the TNC-stacked International Chamber of Commerce. There would be no appeal, similar to the WTO tribunal.

3. Private investors could force governments to change their laws or risk being sued for compensation.

4. No regulative demands whatsoever can be put on corporations or investors. In particular, so-called "performance standards" that would affect foreign investors could become illegal, for example, any requirement that a government agency can only purchase organic foods, recycled paper, or use only renewable energy.

5. Any form of subsidy, aid, grant, or credit given to domestic firms or a particular group, for example, women, would be forbidden unless given to foreign investors as well. Also forbidden, for example, could be the EU support for economically distressed regions.

6. Corporations can demand compensation from governments for lost profit opportunities due to any disturbance to their business, for example, war, consumer boycotts, strikes, civil disturbance. (A convenient way to neutralize the effect of a consumer boycott!)

7. Sanctions or boycotts against other countries for human rights or other political reasons, such as against South Africa in the 1980s or Burma in the 1990s are not permitted. (Nelson Mandela would still be in jail!)

8. A signatory to the Agreement is committed for an incredible *20 years,* as 15 years' notice must be given, and not before the first five years have passed. Obligations to pay compensation for lost profit opportunity would last the whole period.

Notable by glaring absence are any obligations or accountability of the TNCs or investors for *their* actions and policies, for example, their anti-competitive business practices, their unethical behavior, and their treatment of labor, local communities, and the environment.

If the idea for the MAI had been suggested in a science fiction novel, it might at best have been the basis for a B-movie. Most people would consider it too far-fetched to be plausible. But MAI is for *real.* It is happening *now.* And very powerful forces are determined to make it happen, if not in its present form, then in another form. There is already talk on the Internet of plans to have it smuggled into the IMF statutes as a Trojan horse now that the original plans have been exposed.

Lest anyone is in doubt about the seriousness of the MAI threat, the ongoing case of Ethyl Corporation of the USA vs. the Canadian government ought to dispel any doubts about what will happen if and when MAI is implemented. Ethyl Corporation, the world's only manufacturer of a gasoline additive called "MMT," sued Canada for US $251 million under the NAFTA compensation provisions, which are very MAI-like. The background is that Canada banned MMT because it is a suspected neurotoxin with undesirable environmental effects. MMT is already banned in some US states for the same reason. Ethyl Corp.'s claim is that the very act of the Canadian parliament debating an MMT ban constituted an "expropriation of the company's assets." [6]

In a second NAFTA case, the Mexican government protested the dumping of chemical waste in a nature park and was promptly sued by foreign investors for $400 million in compensation for not being allowed to use the park as a toxic dump.[7]

Some observers are now calling this new concept the "paying the polluter" principle, the very reverse of the "polluter pays" principle. Under this incredible MAI principle, the government has to pay compensation if the polluter is not allowed to profit from polluting the environment, and also pays the cleanup bill if the polluter *is* allowed to pollute the environment, in what might be called a "lose-lose" proposition.

The word going around in TNC corridors these days is that the way to make the really *big* money under the coming MAI regime is to have your virtual company announce a new product that is carcinogenic or toxic, and then, when it is banned, demand compensation for lost profit opportunity. You don't even need employees for this strategy—just hordes of lawyers.

If the MAI regime becomes a reality—even in modified form with "national exceptions" (their fallback strategy), the consequences can be predicted fairly accurately, more or less in the following order:

1. Further consolidation of the TNCs into even larger, more powerful entities than we know today, where many are already larger in turnover and wealth than most nation states.
2. Further concentration of wealth in fewer and fewer hands. The gap between rich and poor will widen even more, both within countries and between countries.
3. Acceleration in environmental degradation as the TNCs compete to rape the Earth of its remaining resources as quickly as possible. ("Go out and get those resources while they are still there," as one businessman recently implored a class of business school graduates.)
4. Homogenization of culture globally into a McDonald's/Disneyland/Coca Cola/Time Warner society where attempts to hold on to native customs, language, locally produced food, handicrafts, films, etc., will be challenged as restrictions of trade limiting TNC profits.
5. An increase in terrorism as the only response available to increasingly desperate peoples.
6. A growing resistance to the TNC regime by civil society—boycotts, civil disturbances, and new political movements with demands for reform that will be ignored.
7. Eventually a total breakdown of human society as we know it will occur due to a combination of factors, including civil disturbance, breakdown of ecological support systems, mass starvation, epidemics due to the poisoned environment, terrorism, mass migration due to environmental destruction, and a financial collapse that will

make 1929 look like a warming up exercise, as investors the world over all head for the exit at the same time. Even before the WTO/MAI threat emerged, the international Union of Concerned Scientists predicted such a breakdown by 2020 due to ecological factors alone.[8]

8. This will be followed by a long period that Chief Seattle characterized as "the end of living and the beginning of survival" in his appeal to the white man in 1854. It won't be pretty. A forced return to local food and renewable energy production throughout the globe will happen. A "new start" economy will evolve eventually based on reinstating the ancient value systems of indigenous peoples everywhere, that sees man and nature as inseparably intertwined. Commercial interests will finally be subordinated to community interests by an indignant populace. Sustainable local communities, cultural diversity, political reform, and a new form of global governance based on sharing will be the backbone of a new renaissance. The era of ecovillage will begin in a new solar age. A bitter and expensive lesson will have been learned.

Is there any chance of a "soft landing" that would allow the WTO to be reformed from within? It is still too early to say, but two recent events suggest that there is some flexibility.

The first was the dramatic anti-WTO demonstration in Seattle in late November 1999. This was the first time that we saw a major direct confrontation between the Cultural Creatives and the Moderns, with the CCs as clear winners. The demonstration came as a shock to many people because they were unaware of the breadth of the opposition to the WTO, and unaware of the reasons, as this opposition has been suppressed in the popular media. This is not surprising to anyone who knows that the media are controlled by the commercial corporations, who are not keen on giving the CCs media coverage, thus weakening their own position. Nor is it surprising that the media attempted to explain the demonstrations as the work of irresponsible hooligans, who in fact, were but a very small part of the demonstrations, but the focal point of most American TV coverage. The media did not give much air time to the 100 serious NGOs behind the demonstrations, who were arguing that the WTO was a tool of the commercial corporations, undemocratic, and not in the interest of the people. However, the WTO delegates themselves were well aware of what was happening and its significance. Support was given to the demonstrators by many delegates from the South, whose resistance to the WTO was strengthened, and who called for more democracy in the WTO, a very positive sign. In addition, President Clinton defended their right to be heard, mostly because of organized labor's participation. The WTO is now aware that its every step is going to be watched under a magnifying glass by the world's NGOs, including any attempt to revive MAI, and ordinary people are starting to ask some serious questions as to why they have been kept in the dark about all this until now.

The second positive sign relates to GMO—genetically modified organisms, another example of a debate that has been suppressed or nonexistent in the USA. Until recently. It all started with English housewives who began boycotting supermarkets that were selling GMOs. Their attitude reflected a widespread feeling in Europe that GMOs could be a potential threat to the ecology and to human health, as many biologists have warned. We just do not know enough about the possible serious consequences of messing with the DNA of various organisms. The principle of caution suggests we take things slowly until we know more, while the commercial companies interest is to take the chance that there will be no major problems. When hit on the bottom line, however, the commercial corporations can react fast! Soon all the UK supermarkets, one after another, declared they would not sell GMOs. The same reaction followed quickly in many countries on the continent, and soon it became EU policy to exercise caution with GMOs, regardless of the scientific evidence or commercial consequences. This was a direct challenge to the WTO, whose foundation is built upon the concept that "scientific proof" is required before any product can be banned. In a major negotiation in Montreal early this year, the EU's position on GMOs received majority support among WTO members, against American opposition. This would not have happened without the Seattle demonstrations, and establishes a very important precedent, because it puts the interests of the consumers ahead of the interests of the commercial companies for the first time. Another victory for the Cultural Creatives. Now many Americans are beginning to ask themselves how it is that 80% of their food contains GMOs that the rest of the world finds questionable. Truly an interesting question! Finally the debate begins.

Hopefully, the real pros and cons of the WTO regime will be debated now, and reform from within forced upon the TNCs by the interests of consumers who argue that they have a legitimate right to regulate *for any reason and without scientific proof,* what products are sold in their territories. Will they succeed? No one knows at this stage, and I have my serious doubts, because the opposition of the TNCs, who control the money, the politicians and the media, is going to be enormous.

As an exercise in visioning, let us now take a look at how a post globalization society might look several decades after the crash and a period of rebuilding.

15

The Era of Ecovillage

Imagine now that you are fast-forwarded in time for three generations. You are being permitted by the divine to make a brief visit with your great granddaughter, Anne, in 2064. She lives in an ecovillage near Copenhagen, Denmark.

As you enter the area on a sunny morning in June, you are struck by the flowers and luxurious plant growth, and a small stream running beside the gravel path through a small woods of birch and beech trees. It is very peaceful. Birds are singing. You can see three or four dwellings among the trees. Then there she is, waiting for you, a beautiful, healthy looking girl in her mid-twenties with an easy smile. She is dressed casually in slacks and blouse, with blond, braided hair, sunglasses, and a floppy white hat. You are burning with curiosity and full of questions about what has happened in the intervening years, and can hardly contain yourself.

"Welcome to Ecoville," she says enthusiastically, and gives you a gentle kiss on the cheek. "Let's walk this way. I live a little further down the path. I have arranged for Jonathan to join us, and my husband Robert. Jonathan is the oldest resident, and is good on history. I am afraid I am not too good on pre-crunch times."

"Pre-crunch? What's that?"

"Your time. Before the 'crunch.' That's what we call the big breakdown. 2013 I think. You'll have to ask Jonathan."

"What happened then?"

"That was when the USA decided to join the Gaian League and all hell broke loose. Europe split. The markets crashed. Everything was chaos. Did you ever meet Heidi High? She was terrific. Maybe that was after your time."

"Ummm. No. Don't know the name."

"Was Clinton your time?

"Oh, yes. Indeed. What do people say about him now?"

Anne slowly pouts her lips, and speaks slowly in a low, gravely voice, "Read my lips," then laughs heartily.

"That was Bush."

"Oh. Anyway, I'm more interested in permaculture."

Suddenly, three romping dogs run playfully across the path just ahead of you. You are struck by the weird sight of the odd goggles they have on their heads.

"What are those strange things?" you break out.

"The goggles? That's to protect them from the ozone hole. Otherwise they would go blind. All our domestic animals have them. Many of the wild ones too. Unfortunately, we can't protect them all. And of course they are mandatory for the children. As are caps, long sleeves and trousers. We have a very high incidence of skin cancer here."

"How bad is the hole now?"

"It covers slightly less than half the globe at its peak. It's seasonal, you know. It's worst in New Zealand, Australia, and here in Scandinavia. We estimate it will take another hundred years to return to normal. The good news is that the size of the holes seems to be slowly decreasing now."

"Anne, in that connection, let me ask you. How do people look at my time, the 20th century, from your perspective today?"

Anne frowns deeply. "Frankly, we have great difficulty understanding the mentality. In school history classes, it is called the Age of Greed. We can't understand how people could be so selfish, and could destroy the environment. It's not just the ozone hole. It's everything. The deforestation, the destruction of topsoil, the pesticides in the water, the extinction of so many species, the radioactive wastes, the wars. Actually, worst of all is the endocrine disrupters—the synthetic estrogens in the water and ecosystem from your time. They are still creating havoc with our reproductive systems decades after they were banned. Hundreds of millions of lives have been ruined." She bites her lip and looks down. "Neither Robert nor I can have children."

"Oh, I'm sorry."

Anne bends down and gently lifted up a tiny kitten, whose goggles are on crooked, straightens them, strokes the kitten lovingly, and puts it down again without a word.

You can't help being very touched, and ask: "How do you cope, Anne?"

Anne looks your way for a long time as she seems to be searching for the right words. It's hard to see her eyes through the dark sunglasses. Then she turns her head again. "We just cope," she says, staring straight ahead without expression.

A clearing in the woods exposes a parking area with several small vehicles and a bus. You ask, "What do we have here?"

"Those are our solar vehicles. We use them mostly for shopping in town or for linking onto the sunway into the city."

"The sunway?"

"That's the mass transit system. It's like a continuous, high-speed conveyor belt really. We can get to city center in about ten minutes from here.

"How far is that?"

"About 30 kilometers."

"And it's solar driven?"

"Almost everything is solar driven nowadays. We have come a long way in that area compared to your time. The only limitation is battery capacity. You wouldn't believe how powerful some of them are."

"No gasoline motors?"

"No. No. Only in exceptional cases. Petroleum is too valuable to burn. It's rationed now. Used mostly for pharmaceuticals and special plastics these days."

"Rationed, you say? Who decides that? I am very curious about how decisions are made. And about your government. And what about private companies? What role do they play? And is it the same in other countries?"

"Ummm. That was a mouthful. Well, things are done very differently now. I think Robert would be best at explaining government. He is an economist and the EV rep. But I will try."

"What's that? The EV rep?"

"Well, each ecovillage elects a representative, who is the EV's leader. He represents the EV's interests in the next level of governance, consisting of roughly ten EVs, or 5000 people on average. And so on up. There are seven levels in all, each one roughly ten times larger in population than the lower level. The reps at each level choose one from their midst to represent them at the next level."

"You mean individuals don't vote for politicians?"

"Well, not for a political party. We don't have them anymore. Individuals vote for their EV rep, and in the direct election of our Earth Councilor for our Earth region and in referendums and polls, which are frequent. The seven Earth Councilors form what we call Earth Council, which is the supreme power now. We also vote in the sense that we can prioritize how money should be spent in our local community. The EV reps together form legislative and executive branches at the different levels, depending on their interests and abilities. A Prime Minister of the Gaian League is appointed by the Earth Council from among the EV reps, and he forms a cabinet.

"One of the things that has been most criticized about pre-crunch times was the one-man, one-vote party system. That system encouraged special interest political parties and egotistical voting patterns. It created division instead of unity. No one had a vested interest in protecting the commons. Today, the situation is the opposite. EV reps would never dream of supporting any law that would damage their own local community's environment. If they did, they would be summarily kicked out of office. And so on, all the way up. All politicians have to be EV reps. Even the Gaian League Prime Minister represents an EV."

"Who makes the laws then?"

"The fifth level is bioregions, there are several hundred of those of varying sizes. For example, Denmark is one. They have a lot of autonomy. Together their reps form a global legislature. But there are also regional legislatures, for example, in Earth Regions, bioregions and nation states, with delegated areas of authority that are appropriate for the scale they represent."

"And the EV system is the same all over the world."

"There are a lot of variants, but the basic EV models are quite similar, with emphasis on a high degree of self-sufficiency and strong local communities. There is a high degree of agreement across all racial and cultural groups, because we nurture and respect our differences."

"But surely not everybody can live in ecovillages?" you say.

Anne laughs, "Of course they can. It is simply a question of definition. An EV today is defined as a local community of order of magnitude 500 persons, no matter where you live. They have special rights and obligations according to law, including funding to carry out their tasks. In fact, most are in the cities. This was probably the single most important reform post-crunch. We can thank Heidi High for that."

"Who was this Heidi High?"

"She was the American president that took the USA into the Gaian League in a showdown with the TNCs. The event of the century. She issued the blue dollar and "blue" them away." Anne laughs. "Old joke. Jonathan can tell you more."

"And you don't have political parties anymore?"

"Nope. What is the point? Your parties were a sham, no longer representing the real interests of the people. They were mostly promoting cancerous economic growth and reflecting the interests of the TNCs. But believe me, there is still plenty of room for debate. We don't agree on everything. Besides, it is an easy matter to poll everybody electronically these days."

"Are there still TNCs, then?"

"Yes, some, but they are strictly regulated by the Gaian Trade Organization, which replaced the old WTO, and by the Gaian Charter, which all member states must adhere to. Jonathan can tell you more when we see him. Is there anything particular you would like to see first?"

You say, "Well, I would love to see an inner city ecovillage if there is time. Would that be possible?"

"Sure. We can do that now. Then come back. It will only take a few minutes. Come. We can take this solar car here."

After a short drive in the silent and comfortable car, you approach a sign saying "Sunway approach. Drive 170 kph."

"Here we hit the approachway and go onto automatic pilot. This way collisions are impossible. It will automatically merge us with the sunway in about one minute. I have requested an exit in an inner city area that used to be our worst slum quarter."

You find yourselves soon on an elevated enclosed multilane beltway with many vehicles around you and a panoramic view to both sides, mostly residential areas with clusters of low buildings, but getting higher as you approach the city. After a few minutes your attention is caught by a huge white flower-like object dominating the skyline in the distance. "What is that over there, Anne?"

"You are looking at Earth Center, home of the Earth Council and headquarters of the Gaian League."

"It's beautiful."

"A few years ago there was an international competition for the best design for a new Earth Center. This was the winner, called 'the lotus', modeled on the sacred thousand-petaled flower. There is one petal for each bioregion on the planet."

"What a wonderful idea!"

You stare in silence together at the marvelous structure until it begins to recede again. Then Anne says, "It is spectacular from the air. I can arrange a flyover for you later if you like."

"I would love that."

Soon you are moved into a slower lane and whisked off the sunway onto an exit belt, clearly near the center of the city as high rises dominate the immediate area. Soon Anne is maneuvering in light city traffic, until she pulls into a parking area. "This dead end street you see here is an inner city ecovillage called EV Bygholm. Let's have a look."

Twelve buildings, each six stories high, are seen, six on each side of the street, with open space at the end of the street, where a small park area with high trees, tennis courts, a swimming pool, and a children's playground is located. Anne says, "Note the glass structures built onto the south facades. This is an old but effective retrofitting technique for creating the possibility of vegetable gardens for each apartment, even in older buildings like these, which are 200 years old. They are about fifteen meters square. Some use them for an extra room instead. The passive solar effect cuts heating bills also. The roof is also used for growing vegetables in some of these high rises."

You comment, "This looks very orderly. Did you say it used to be a slum?"

"Yes. But the people now take great pride in the area, because they have a big say in what goes on. The key change was to give them responsibilities and the resources to deal with the tasks they were assigned. This particular EV takes care of a number of retarded children and adults from the city, who are full-fledged members of their community. That was the majority wish. Each EV usually has a particular mission. We call it the 'glue' that keeps them together. People can choose almost any kind of EV they want in the inner city. Some are spiritually-based. Some, like this one, have a social function. Some are for retirees. Some are just friends, who got together. Some contract to run schools or other public facilities. We have found that delegating social and other tasks to the EVs saves tremendous costs compared to the old central-planned welfare state with its cumbersome institutions.

"An important thing in the inner city is to create a food market and shopping area for daily needs within walking distance for everyone, normally maximum one km. This cuts down drastically on traffic, and helps create community. This EV shares such a shopping center with two others in the adjoining block. In this case, it is an indoor mall in one of the other buildings a little further down the road. The outside facilities are common, and their use is determined by the EVs themselves. They are given limited public funds for their commons. They can also influence what projects are done in their areas by voting a portion of their tax money. This one apparently likes tennis. There are many variants. Cars are normally kept in one place on the perimeter, so the children can play on the street. But they can drive in occasionally when necessary.

"Most big cities the world over now have similar arrangements. We and others have found that this kind of structure drastically reduces costs, inner city crime and family break-ups, and most important, creates thriving local communities. At the same time, people express a much greater satisfaction with their lives when they feel they are part of a network and can jointly influence their immediate surroundings."

It is soon time to go back to Ecoville. After a quick return trip past the Earth Center, you find yourself again walking through the woods with Anne, who says shortly, "This is where I live."

She leads you through a beautifully kept vegetable garden to her home, a relatively small white brick dwelling with small windows and a roof of classic red tile with about six square meters of solar heaters. As with the other homes in the woods, you note that there are no fences or lawns around the house, only paths with a variety of different plants and rock gardens on either side. Inside, the impression is very pleasing, with a cool tile floor and a sculptured white brick Finnish stove in the center of the dining and kitchen area.

Anne says, "The combination of the Finnish stove for the winter and solar heaters for warm water in the summer is the preferred energy solution for our climate. We are self sufficient in energy with just the small willow wood you saw outside. The stove is 95% efficient and we built it ourselves. We share it with two other couples, but each couple has its own private quarters. The walls are compressed earth bricks taken from the site here by a local craftsman. It is low cost and gives a very nice indoors climate as the walls can 'breathe.' The windows are standard triple thermal, and the wood is all local pine. We have to be much more cost conscious than in your day. And more conscious about using local materials and labor because of the "true cost" accounting system we now use. The technology is actually quite old, but effective. Incidentally, most ecovillages today, including ours, are about 70 to 80 percent self-sufficient in food, even in the cities. Here is my husband, Robert."

Robert appears in a doorway and offers his hand to you. He is tall, well dressed, with freckles, reddish hair and a healthy outdoor look.

"Hi. I understand you are an economist?" you say. "What do economists do these days?"

"Well, I do research and teaching. The 'true cost accounting' concept that Anne mentioned is certainly the main area of research, and has been for many years. The Gaian Charter requires us to internalize all the indirect social and environmental costs of products sold on our markets, as required in classical economics, but, as you probably know, blatantly ignored in your time. It gives us a completely different picture of what things really cost compared to pre-crunch. But it is not a simple thing to do in practice. There are many controversies, and we economists debate the pros and cons of different theories and ways to measure things."

"So what have the main effects been of introducing these 'true costs'?"

"There are several," replies Robert. "One is a major shift back to natural products away from synthetics. Synthetics are simply devastating to the ecosystem, and hence to our health costs. They cannot be justified except in a few special cases where there are no viable substitutes. Another is a drastic reduction in international trade and a flowering of local businesses and local communities all over the world. We see today a net flow of people away from the megacities into the villages from which they came in the last century, particularly in the South. That is where the jobs are today. One result of this is a quantum leap in the quality of life the world over. Standards of living are much higher today by our measures, although your economists might claim they were lower because consumption is lower. However, we think your way of measuring things was rather screwed up, for example your Gross National Product, which was a mixture of positive and negative contributors to quality of life."

"And population is much higher, I assume?"

"No. Population is actually lower today than at the turn of the century. Not so much because it was planned that way, but because of widespread epidemics and the fact that so many people in this century have been born sterile or suffered from deformities of the reproductive organs due to endocrine disrupters in the ecosystem. These are estrogen-like synthetics that often confuse and damage the fetus during pregnancy. They have been banned for decades, but are incredibly widespread and robust. They will continue to be a major health and social problem for us well into the next century."

At that moment, a rangy, elderly gentleman, with a graying, close-cropped beard, and looking very fit, parks his bicycle outside the window on the terrace and enters the room, taking off his sunglasses. Anne exclaims, "Here comes Jonathan, one of our elders—the one I mentioned to you who has studied pre-crunch history. He even experienced some of it personally as a young man."

"Nice to meet you, Jonathan. I am curious about the Gaian League that Anne mentioned. Would you would be the right person to tell me about what it is and how it came about.?"

"Sure. The Gaian League today includes all of the nations on this planet, but that is very recent. For many decades, China was a holdout, and tried to follow its own path based on pre-crunch values. But their experiment ended in environmental disaster, and the world community is now helping them rebuild. The League members are all bound by the Gaian Charter and are members of the GTO, the Gaian Trade Organization. The special feature of the Gaian Charter is that members must declare their first loyalty to the planet as a whole, even ahead of their own nation state. This was seen early on by its founders as the only way to break the vicious circle of greed and exploitation, and screw your neighbor policies that were destroying the planet's ecosystem at the beginning of the century, mostly because politicians had ceded power to the TNCs and were wedded to the fantasy of never-ending economic growth."

"And who were the founders?"

"Well, the initiator was an odd fellow," says Jonathan smiling, as they all exchange glances, chuckling at what seems to be a private joke.

"Sorry. That was actually his name, Odd Fellow Hansen, the maverick prime minister of Denmark that took Denmark out of the WTO and the European Union in '06, and formed the Gaian League and the GTO along with Norway, Iceland, Sweden and Holland, the latter two also leaving the EU. He is something of a folk hero here."

"A legend," adds Anne.

"How did that come about?"

"The Danish people were furious with the actions of the TNCs, who were suing them for billions in lost profits because the Danes had banned endocrine disrupters. The people in several other countries of Europe, the Americas, and the South were also angry with the TNCs. But the Danish students were the first to take civil action. They occupied the Folketing, demanding the resignation of the government and withdrawal from the WTO and the MAI."

Anne interrupts, "Jonathan is too modest to say it, but he was one of the student leaders."

"That doesn't matter," mumbles Jonathan a little shyly. He continues: "Anyway, Odd Fellow was a highly respected civil servant, who was brought in to carry out the reforms, which he did with a hard hand. Thus the Gaian League was born. Initially, it was very small and insignificant. But it was a resounding success, both economically and in every other way. The people were empowered with a new vision that was meaningful. It was incredible to experience that energy. The turning point came when the Germans left the EU and joined the League after much debate. That provoked a constitutional crisis in the USA, who were on the brink of civil war over the issue before Heidi High brought the USA into the Gaian League also. The rest is history. Others followed quickly. An era was over—a new one began. Today, Europe is reunited and thriving as never before."

"Quite a story. Can you tell me more about the Gaian Charter?" you ask.

"Sure," says Jonathan. "The Gaian Charter builds heavily on the Earth Charter, which emerged out of the Rio summit in 1992, and was first finalized several years later. However, there are some important additions which put more teeth into the Gaian Charter. One, as I mentioned, is the requirement that members swear their first loyalty to the planet, even ahead of their home nation. It led eventually to the concept of the Earth Council. It was tough for many nations to accept, because it meant trusting in the "wise men" of the Earth Council to protect their vital interests. The second was an extension of human rights to cover clean water, soil, and air, with enforceable sanctions on governments that did not comply. The third was the requirement to internalize all environmental and social costs in market prices, what we now call 'total cost accounting.' Finally, the Charter established the Gaian Trade Organization as an alternative to the old WTO for any nations who wished to join."

"And what were its major differences from the WTO?"

Robert picks up the ball, continuing, "The GTO, as it came to be known, turned the WTO principles upside down. Corporations and private investors were given few rights, but many obligations and responsibilities, while government rights, particularly local community rights, were substantially strengthened. A key provision was a return to the original concept of a corporate charter as a privilege extended by a nation state, and not a right. Under GTO rules, a company's charter can be removed without compensation if it fails to live up to its obligations, and this happened a lot in the early days. They are required to respect the restrictions on their activities and products in the markets where they operate. Your economists would call this protection of inefficient local producers. This is true in a few cases and we have procedures to minimize abuse. However, in general, we see local culture, customs, language and community infrastructure as legitimate things to protect from outside commercial exploitation."

"So the supreme power to settle disputes is now in the hands of a seven-person Earth Council, I understand. How are they chosen, and what powers do they have?"

"They are chosen by direct election in each Earth Region, and they choose a chairman from their midst. For example, Europe is one Earth Region. There are very special qualifications required to be eligible. They have to have demonstrated throughout their lives a dedication to the planet Earth and the values of the Gaian charter in some way or other. They function as a council of wise men and women, resolving any conflicts that cannot be resolved peacefully elsewhere. Their loyalty has to be to the planet and not their region. They are not necessarily politicians. Historically, many have been poets, scientists, philosophers, human and social rights activists, and much more. They act with joint powers similar to the president of one of your 20th century republics. They can appoint and remove the Prime Minister of the Gaian League and put forth guidelines that the legislative and executive branches must follow."

"And they control the military?"

"Yes," says Robert. "They have the power to intervene militarily if necessary. But it is a very rare occurrence. No region has its own military any more, only a police force. You can imagine how much money we save compared to your time. One thing which made this development possible was that nobody could afford military expenses anymore. That is why it is so important to choose the right kind of people for Earth Council, namely persons who have no egos, no personal agenda, and much love for their fellow man. The whole system is based ultimately on trust that our Earth Councilors will do the right thing. The people have seldom been disappointed. It actually works."

Anne speaks up, "We have been doing a project on Earth Council in the school the last few weeks. If you like, we could wander over and hear from the children."

You respond, "Let's do that. I'd love to hear more about your school system."

You leave Anne and Robert's house, and walk further into the village. Anne explains: "Most ecovillages have their own nurseries and primary schools up to grade nine. Some combine with a neighboring EV if they are too small. We see it as vital to link the learning process with life in the local community. These days, a lot of the more routine learning can be self-taught on the Net with excellent self-teach programs and holographic teachers. Our task at the school is to teach values, research techniques and problem solving rather than rote learning. We do this through relevant projects from the real world, often with several age groups together. The older kids help a lot with the younger ones. It is a quite different concept from that of your time. And the kids start doing it very young."

"And what are the values you teach?" you ask.

"Most EVs agree on the most fundamental values, although there are variations of emphasis. The most common system builds on what we call the 'five pillars'—peace, truth, love, right livelihood, and non-violence, based on the teachings of Sai Baba and Sai Prem. In addition, we emphasize the value system of indigenous peoples, who see Man as an intrinsic part of nature. Many of the troubles of your time stemmed directly from the erroneous idea that nature was a resource separate from Man. We teach children ecology and permaculture from the earliest age. They learn that if they harm nature, they harm themselves. They are constantly reminded of this by their ozone goggles."

As the group approaches the schoolhouse, several children bearing goggles and peaked caps are seen working outside the building. Anne explains: "This is an example of practical learning. The children are learning by building a straw bale house from local materials. It is now a very common construction technique in many parts of the world. Later they will teach the technique to other children in other countries with whom they communicate on the Net. Each EV has a number of 'twins' in different parts of the world. They are in constant contact and visit each other as part of their education. That trip is in fact the highlight of the year. This autumn they are going to China for three months, and they spent much of their time learning about China and preparing for the trip."

The group walks into the schoolhouse where they quickly find a group of children of various ages sitting quietly in a big circle with their teacher, Marie, a competent-looking middle-aged woman.

After brief introductions, Anne continues: "Marie here has been working with the children on an Earth Council project the last two weeks. Would you like to tell us something about it, Marie?"

"I'd be delighted, Anne. When we heard about your visit, the older children were very excited and wanted to study about your times in the archives, which they have been doing very diligently. Their assignment was to find people from your time that they think would have made good Earth Councilors if such had existed at that time. Each child is doing a report to the class on his or her choice. Shall we do a round, kids, and you tell our guests whom you chose and why, just very briefly?" The children nod. "OK. Tell us your choices for the seven councilors in the late 20th century?" She nods to one of the older boys, about fifteen, who starts the round.

He stands up and speaks up proudly as if he has found a gem, "Nelson Mandela, South Africa, because he fought for his people's rights and was incorruptible." He remains standing.

The next, a girl about the same age, rises and says, "Wangari Matthai, Kenya, because she gave pride to the women of Africa and taught them to plant trees."

A younger girl is next. She joins the two standing and says, "Thomas Berry, United States, because of his Story of the Universe, and his passion for the Earth."

The boy beside her rises and pipes up strongly, "Mikhael Gorbachov, Russia, because he tore down the iron curtain dividing Europe."

A dark complexioned young girl is next, "Vandana Shiva, because she exposed the 'green revolution' as a disastrous policy for the poor people of India."

A boy of about 13 adds, "Bill Mollison, Australia, because he invented permaculture."

An Asiatic-looking young girl rises, and says: "Wei Jingsheng, for his fight for democracy in China and his writings 'The Courage to Stand Alone'."

"And who is your choice for chairman?" asks Marie.

The children have obviously rehearsed, as they exchange glances and say in one voice, "Nelson Mandela." The first boy is beaming. Then they take their places again.

"Well, there you are," says Marie. "I wonder if they would have made a difference if they had been given the power? Food for thought, eh?"

Anne chips in: "How about the younger children? I understand they have an assignment too."

"Yes," says Marie. "The third to seventh graders were asked to choose someone from *anytime* in the past, someone they can relate to who would have been a prime candidate for Earth Council in his or her time. Of course, we help them a little, but they are all very good at searching the web. They have to imagine they were that person, and make a report back to the group about what they did to make this a better world. Shall we ask them? OK, kids, just tell us the name this time. Who are you going to be?"

The younger children, from about 9-12 years, pipe up in turn:

"Francis Bacon."

"Mohammed."

"Odd Fellow."

"Buddha."

"Mahatma Ghandi."

"Giordano Bruno."

"Heidi High."

"Thomas Jefferson"

"Confucius."

"Jesus of Nazareth."

"Well!" says Marie, "A mixed bag, but quite impressive."

A little pre-schooler, about five, somebody's little sister, pipes up: "I want to be Heidi High."

Marie says to her gently: "Sweetie, we *have* a Heidi High already."

The little girl starts to cry: "I said it first," she sobs.

Marie puts her arm around her, "OK, Sweetie, you sit with Karen over there and you can *both* be Heidi High. OK, Karen?"

You get inspired to ask the little girl a question, "And what are you going to be when you grow up?"

"An Earthmother," she says with a slight frown.

You look over to Jonathan quizzically. All these new expressions!

Jonathan explains: "The young staff who work for the Earth Council are called Earthmothers and Earthmen. It is considered a great honor to be selected, and competition is fierce. It is a bit like a combination of the old UN and the Peace Corp." He turns to the 5-year old and says sternly, "Then you are going to have to study very hard, young lady."

"I will," she says determinedly.

"We may have another Heidi High in the making here," says Jonathan with wide eyes, as he looks up, smiling.

And so, your visiting time is about up almost before it began. There are so many questions you didn't get to ask. You all thank Marie and the children. You say your good-byes to Robert and Jonathan with a gentle hug, and head back to the entrance where you came in with Anne, towards a strange-looking disk waiting near the entrance.

"You will get a nice view of the lotus today, I'm sure," says Anne. "Well, I hope you had a nice visit," she adds sweetly. "It was much too short." She pauses, "I won't ask you if you would rather live in our time or your own."

You reach out and give her a gigantic hug, and with a sly smile, say: "Because you know you don't have to ask." and head for the disk.

On an impulse, you turn, and add, "I guess I was very fortunate that you happened to live here. This is the world capital now, isn't it?."

"I suppose so, although we don't call it that. Earth Center is certainly here. Just a quirk of history, I guess, because of Odd Fellow," says Anne thoughtfully.

"Or because of Jonathan and his student friends," you add.

You wave goodbye as you enter the disk and are soon gliding over the giant lotus that dominates the whole city seen from the sky. The new symbol of global unity is every bit as spectacular as Anne said it would be.

It is time to return now as you climb further and further towards the stars until the lotus is just a white speck far below, and the roundness of the horizon is now apparent. Your last thought is of Anne and her friends: "The Earth is in good hands."

Notes

Chapter 2   Environmental Crisis
1. Barry Commoner, *The Closing Circle* (New York: Alfred A. Knopf, 1971)
2. Donella H. Meadows, Dennis L. Meadows, Jørgen Randers, William W. Behrens III, *The Limits to Growth* (London: Earth Island Limited, 1972)
3. Jay W. Forrester, *World Dynamics* (Cambridge, Mass.: Wright-Allen Press, 1971)
4. Thomas S. Kuhn, *The Structure of Scientific Revolutions* (Chicago: University of Chicago Press, 1962)

Chapter 4   Muktananda
1. JT Ross Jackson, *Kali Yuga Odyssey: A Spiritual Journey* (San Francisco, Robert D. Reed Publishers, 2000)

Chapter 8   Gaia Trust
1. Corinne McLaughlin and Gordon Davidson, *Builders of the Dawn* (Shutesbury, Massachusetts, Sirius Publishing, 1986)

Chapter 9   Green Technologies
1. E.F. Schumacher, *Small is Beautiful: Economics As If People Mattered* (Harper Collins, 1989).

Chapter 10   The Global Ecovillage Network
1. Robert & Diane Gilman (Context Institute), *Ecovillages and Sustainable Communities: A Report for Gaia Trust* (private circulation, Gaia Trust, 1991)
2. David Korten, *When Corporations Rule the World* (London: Earthscan Publications, 1995)
3. See www.gaia.org

Chapter 11   A New Culture Emerges
1. Hanne Norup Carlsen, JT Ross Jackson, Niels I Meyer, editors, *When No Means Yes; Danish Visions of a Different Europe* (London, Adamantine Press, 1992)
2. Paul H. Ray, *"The Integral Culture Survey: A Study of the Emergence of Transformational Value in America"* (study paper sponsored by Fetzer Institute and The Institute of Noetic Sciences, 1996)

Chapter 12   Shareholder Protectionism
1. Herman Daly, *"Free Trade: The Perils of Deregulation,"* in Jerry Mander and Edward Goldsmith, editors, *The Case Against the*

Global Economy (San Francisco, Sierra Club Books, 1996), p.232
2. Adam Smith, *The Wealth of Nations* (1776, reprinted by Pelican Books, 1977)
3. Chief Seattle, version of his speech from 1854 according to www.nidlink.com/%7Ebobhard/seattle.htm
4. Herman Daly, *"Sustainable Growth? No Thank You,"* in Mander and Goldsmith (see 1), p193
5. PM Vitousek et. al., *"Human Appropriation of the Products of Photosynthesis,"* Bioscience 37(4), 1986
6. Nasser Saber, *Speculative Capital: Volume 1* (London, Financial Times/Prentice Hall, 1999), p.160
7. David Korten, *The Post-Corporate World: Life After Capitalism* (San Francisco, Berrett-Koehler/Kumarian Press, 1999)
8. Tim Lang and Colin Hines, *The New Protectionism* (London, Earthscan Publications, 1993)

Chapter 13   World Government: Part 1
1. Ralph Nader and Lori Wallach, *"GATT, NAFTA, and the Subversion of the Democratic Process,"* in Mander and Goldsmith, p.99
2. ibid, p.93
3. ibid, p.94
4. ibid, p.95
5. ibid, p.95
6. ibid, p.98
7. The Ecologist (July/August, 1997), p. 137
8. Reference 1 above, p.106
9. ibid, p. 101

Chapter 14   World Government: Part 2
1. Paul Hellyer, *The Evil Empire: Globalization's Darker Side* (Canada, Chimo Media, 1997)
2. Quoted on www.greenecon.org/MA, *"MAI: Democracy for Sale"*
3. See www.citizen.org/pctrade/testimony.htm
4. Tony Clarke and Maude Barlow, *The Multilateral Agreement on Investment and the Threat to American Freedom* (Canada, Stoddart Publishers, 1998)
5. ibid, preface
6. Lori Wallach, March 5, 1998, testimony before The House Committee on International Relations Subcommittee of International Economic Policy and Trade
7. Syb Bouma, *An MAI without Gentleness,* Silance (March 1998).
8. See www.ucsusa.org

About the Author

J.T. Ross Jackson is a Canadian-born naturalized Danish citizen living in Copenhagen with his wife Hildur. They have three sons, Rolf, Thor and Fry. Ross earned his B.Sc. in Engineering Physics at Queen's University in Canada, and did his post-graduate studies in the United States, where he received his M.S. in Industrial Management at Purdue University and his Ph.D. in Operations Research at Case Western Reserve University.

What started as a visit to Denmark to get some international business experience in 1964 ended in a permanent move after he met Hildur. Most of his professional career has been as an independent consultant on operations research, with a specialty in software development for financial institutions. In 1987, his long-standing interest in the environment and spirituality resulted in the founding, with Hildur and other Danish friends, of Gaia Trust—a charitable association that supports persons and organizations that are working for the transition to a sustainable planet. He has been chair of the group since that time. Gaia Trust is funded by commercial subsidiary Gaiacorp, which manages currency-based hedge funds and advises international financial institutions on foreign exchange management out of Dublin, Ireland, based on theories and software developed originally by Ross in the early 1980s.

Gaia Trust has given grants to over 80 ecological projects in 20 countries and has invested substantially in small "green" businesses in Denmark. Gaia Trust's main project to date has been the establishment and support of GEN—the Global Ecovillage Network, an international network of ecovillages, which are working models of sustainable living for the new millennium, integrating ecological, social and spiritual aspects into a holistic lifestyle.